SOCIAL STUDIES
FOR
YOUNG ADOLESCENTS:
Programs for Grades 7, 8, and 9

JULIAN C. ALDRICH, *New York University*

EUGENE COTTLE, *University of Wyoming*

Co-Editors

NATIONAL COUNCIL FOR THE SOCIAL STUDIES

A Department of the National Education Association

1201 Sixteenth Street, North West, Washington, D. C. 20036

Third Edition, 1967

Price $2.25

Foreword

The junior high years are increasingly important years. Records seem to indicate that youth is maturing earlier. More girls, for example, are now marrying at age 18 than ever before. Other statistics, more unfortunate, are also moving downward—such as ages of drivers in automobile accidents, as well as the age brackets for many criminal activities. Youth of the junior high age, whether in a junior high or in some other institutional pattern of schooling, are certainly on the threshhold of maturity. It is an exciting, as well as a very important, time.

A review of the literature of professional education, however, shows a dearth of attention to this period of development insofar as schools go. The junior high is frequently lost in a limbo between the treatment of the elementary school which focuses upon the earlier years and attention to the senior high with its concern for the older adolescent. The school program at this critical juncture should provide a valuable orientation to the approaching adult world; unfortunately it is often somewhat of a sterile encounter with removed and seemingly inconsequential subject matter. The junior high program needs to be attuned to current knowledge and developments.

Recent studies in political socialization, for example, reveal the 7th to 9th grade period as a crucial one for capitalizing on the mounting socio-civic concerns of youth. The teachers of these soon-to-be adults have a great responsibility as they plan the prime generalization to be emphasized, select the skills and attitudes to be engendered, and provide the kinds of learning experiences essential at this transitional stage of life. Some of our most sensitive approaches and intricate strategies are needed here. All-important personal characteristics are also given a near-final mold through formal education at this stage, as youth will be less amenable to adult direction and more inclined to accept peer leadership in the years immediately ahead.

All of this poses a considerable challenge to social studies educators as to pertinent curricula and the most timely instructional means, as well as from the standpoint of guidance. The elementary school helps set directions and patterns; the junior high school helps shape and solidify conclusive elements of personality and character.

In this volume, for which we thank editors Aldrich and Cottle and their collaborators, they have again contributed a helpful summary of fundamental insights about youth in this crucial age-range and a variety of school programs which can serve as yardsticks towards excellence. Here are some guidelines for teachers and curriculum workers as they continue to evolve what promise to be the most pertinent and effective programs and procedures, enabling adolescents to grow into the responsible maturity all of us so desperately desire for them.

Richard E. Gross, *President*
National Council for the Social Studies

Preface

The Curriculum Committee of the National Council for the Social Studies has included a volume on the junior high school in its Curriculum Series since 1951. Since the last revision was in 1957, the Committee judged that a new look at the program of the junior high school grades was warranted. The statement in the first edition, "Between the time of the report of the Committee of Ten and today there has been a ferment and some confusion," is still true today. The ferment is of a new kind, and the confusion is caused by many factors. Many schools have faculties who have attempted to apply the findings of recent psychological research by organizing content in terms of the needs and interests of the whole person. Faculties have explored the new content of scholars, including the "non-Western world," to utilize it more effectively. Teachers and scholars have sought to identify major concepts and areas of generalization in order to promote more effective understanding and better critical thinking.

At the same time, the junior high school grades have been affected by limiting factors. State legislation and state education department regulations have questioned the emphasis of junior high school courses in the social studies. The requirement of American history and the legislation of a chronological approach are not unknown. There has been a questioning of the social studies emphasis in some cases, advocating the separate teaching of disciplines. While there have been radical approaches to the teaching of science, mathematics, and foreign language, there have been serious questions about changing the social studies too rapidly. Added to this must be mentioned the tendency to be satisfied with the changes of the 1930s and the 1940s, even by young, new teachers.

The present volume presents points of view about the function of the junior high school as it serves the young adolescent and includes proposals for the improvement of instruction in the junior high school years. While most social studies teachers agree that improvement is needed in the junior high experience, there is no consensus regarding its nature. How should the cultural developments of recent decades be recognized in terms significant to the young adolescent? Should the junior high school present a subject matter that anticipates sequential content in the senior high school, or should it serve the young adolescent in his present environment? What selection of content should be made from a discipline and how should the goals of the school be determined and described? To what extent should the goals of education in the young adolescent years be set by the needs of adult society? Some of these points of discussion arise from the method of instruction, such as textbook recitation in contrast to a method that seeks to develop concepts and generalizations relevant to the contemporary scene. Some of these points arise from a critical examination of the organization of social studies courses and their relation to the total school program.

As a contribution to curriculum investigation this volume presents brief statements regarding the young adolescent in mid-century society and the function of junior high school social studies as the field serves the development of the young adolescent. Social studies programs from selected schools are included to explore some of the questions pertinent to the organization and teaching of the social studies, such as:

1. What are the goals of junior high school education in the social studies and how are these goals determined?
2. To what extent is pupil-teacher planning evident in social studies programs?
3. How does the content of the social studies at

the junior high school level relate to the total Kindergarten-12th grade sequence?

4. How are the procedures of guiding learning experiences carried out?

The programs presented in this volume are based on information received from schools selected from among several whose programs were presented for consideration. The particular purpose and needs of this volume determined the final selection of schools. The programs presented in Section Two are from the University School of Southern Illinois University, Carbondale; from Setauket Junior High School, Setauket, New York; from McPherson Junior High School in Vancouver, Washington; from Robinson Junior High School in Wichita, Kansas; and from the University School, Laramie, Wyoming.

Both co-editors shared in the planning, evaluation, and presentation of this volume. The second co-editor carried on the correspondence, did the revision of the articles, wrote parts of the unsigned descriptions in Section Two, and is solely responsible for the signed article presented as Section Three.

The co-editors express their deep appreciation to the contributors whose professional spirit and dynamic leadership are here expressed. Thanks are due to many others who have offered suggestions and guided the editors in the search for material to present here. Especial thanks must be given to those who have read the manuscript, offered suggestions, and served as liaison with the Curriculum Committee and the National Council: Ruby Crowe, Nelda Davis, Ruth Ellsworth, Dorothy M. Fraser, Helen M. Garrett, Merrill F. Hartshorn, and Edward Swanson.

JULIAN C. ALDRICH,
EUGENE COTTLE, *Editors*

Table of Contents

SECTION ONE

THE JUNIOR HIGH SCHOOL: A SCHOOL FOR THE YOUNG ADOLESCENT

SECTION TWO

SAMPLE PROGRAMS OF SOCIAL STUDIES INSTRUCTION

SECTION THREE

MEETING THE CHALLENGE OF SOCIAL STUDIES INSTRUCTION IN THE JUNIOR HIGH SCHOOL

Section I

The Junior High School:
A School for the Young Adolescent

Chapter 1

The Response of the Young Adolescent to Present-Day Culture

William T. Gruhn
Professor of Education
The University of Connecticut
Storrs, Connecticut

There are a number of developments in American society today that are of direct concern to the young adolescent. Because the adolescent—like people at any other age level—is a part of the society in which he lives, his attitudes, behavior, and development will reflect that society. In some ways the culture of which he is a part will influence the adolescent primarily as an individual, while in other ways it may be reflected in the behavior of adolescents as an age group.

The response of young adolescents to the culture of today frequently appears to be a negative one. This is understandable, because the negative aspects of behavior receive the most attention, especially from adults who do not recall similar behavior on their part as adolescents. Negative behavior is publicized in newspapers, on radio and television, in churches, and even in the schools. But there is much that is positive in the response of adolescents to the culture of which they are a part. The positive as well as the negative aspects of adolescent behavior should receive consideration in any discussion of the subject.

Urbanization of Society

The trend toward urbanization in our society has had as great an impact on today's culture as any other single factor. In 1950, about one in every two youths (ages 10 to 17) was living in urban areas; in 1960, two of every three youths were in urban areas; and in 1970 it is estimated that this will be three of every four youths. For non-white youths the increase has been greater than for white youths.[1] In a few years, an urban belt will extend from Portland, Maine, to Richmond, Virginia, and eventually to Miami, Florida. Elsewhere in the United States there are similar developments, with the rapid growth of cities throughout the Middle West, the Southwest, and the West. At the same time, in the rural areas of the great West, there are actually vacant houses as the small family farm gives way to the merger of this industry into larger enterprises.

With the trend toward urbanization has come increasing mobility of families. The old established families leave large homes in the cities to move to the suburbs. They are replaced in the city by people from rural areas, often from distant states, and several of these families crowd into houses previously occupied by one.

The mobility of the family has probably contributed to the breakdown of the home and family unit. Frequently young people with little education and limited vocational skills move into the old urban centers, leaving behind parents and other relatives who in the past have given continuity and stability to families, even though they were economically poor and culturally limited. Furthermore, the family which moves to the city usually

---

[1] Perlman, Richard, *Statistical Aspects of Antisocial Behavior of the Minor in the United States.* Washington: Children's Bureau, United States Department of Health, Education, and Welfare, December, 1963.

is one which is unemployed. Frequently it is a family in which one parent has left or where some member has had serious personal problems or is in conflict with the law. In the new location, such families may for some time be unemployed, they may be slow in affiliating with a church, and they will not have loyalties to schools, community organizations, nor the city or state in which they now live—loyalties which are necessary to give stability to the life of neighborhoods and communities.

Young adolescents frequently belong to such mobile families. They are influenced by instability in the home and neighborhood, the absence of wholesome family restraints, and a lack of loyalties to established institutions in general and the community in particular. In a study of the experience of junior high school principals with their students, more than two-thirds of the respondents indicated that broken homes present a more serious problem for young adolescents than a decade ago, while less than one per cent reported that this problem is less serious.[2] Furthermore, principals from 65 per cent of the schools reported that conflicts in family relationships present a more serious problem than in the past. In the opinion of these junior high school principals, therefore, young adolescents are facing more difficult problems in their homes than was true a few years ago. The mobility of our population and the trend toward urbanization undoubtedly accentuate those problems among young adolescents.

Juvenile delinquency among young adolescents likewise is influenced considerably by the current trend toward urbanization. In one half of the junior high schools in the United States, according to the principals, juvenile delinquency among young adolescents is more serious than it was 10 years ago, while in only 7 per cent of the schools is this problem less serious. Delinquency becomes a problem among young adolescents because at this age they begin to circulate in a community beyond their own neighborhoods, with less supervision from parents, other relatives, and friends.

According to the 1964 report on crime in the United States, issued by J. Edgar Hoover, Director of the Federal Bureau of Investigation, the arrests among youth increase rather sharply for certain offenses after age 12, reaching their peak by ages 15 and 16.[3] The crimes most prominent at ages 12 to 16 include burglary, larceny, auto theft, vandalism, and runaways. Arrests for such crimes among young adolescents are much higher in cities and suburban areas than in rural communities. In rural communities the sharp increase in such crimes is delayed until ages 15 and 16. Increased delinquency seems to be, therefore, one form of response of young adolescents to the rapid urbanization in our society.

Tension Between Ethnic Groups

The serious tensions that have developed between ethnic groups in many communities can hardly escape the attention of young adolescents. These tensions are frequently aggravated by the mobility of our population. As adults move to new urban neighborhoods they may go through an extended period of adjustment. Frequently they are unemployed, they must form new associations with neighbors and friends, and they may delay in associating themselves with a church and other community organizations.

Tensions between ethnic groups have not been confined to heavily populated areas. Racial integration, especially in the schools, has become a problem in rural as well as in urban areas. Furthermore, members of some nationality groups have moved by the thousands to find employment in rural areas in some of our southern and western states. Migrant workers have contributed to cultural tensions in some rural areas. Young adolescents cannot remain apart from the tensions that have developed among various cultural groups.

The experience of junior high school principals with young adolescents in the tensions between cultural groups has been a reasonably favorable one. Almost half of the principals indicated that there has been little or no change in such tensions during the past 10 years. Only 20 per cent of the principals stated that such tensions have become more serious, while 15 per cent reported that they are less serious. It must be recognized, of course, that many young adolescents attend schools in communities where such problems have not become serious among adults. In fact, at a time when racial tensions in some areas have reached the most explosive stage in our history, other areas have seemed largely free of such problems. Even

---

[2] These data and others in this chapter not credited to another source are based on a comprehensive survey of junior high school education made in 1964 by William T. Gruhn and Harl R. Douglass and to be published in a revision of the book by the authors, *The Modern Junior High School*. New York: The Ronald Press Company.

[3] *Crime in the United States: Uniform Crime Reports—1964.* Issued by J. Edgar Hoover, Director, Federal Bureau of Investigation, United States Department of Justice. Washington: Superintendent of Documents, Government Printing Office, 1965.

so, one might have expected a sharper increase in tensions among adolescent youth of different cultural backgrounds than that reported by junior high school principals.

Demand for More Education

One of the prominent characteristics of our culture today is the sharply increased demand for more education by youth. This demand has come in part from the decline in employment opportunities for those with less than a high school education, as well as from a sharp increase in the positions for which more education or a specific skill is demanded. The aspirations of parents for their children concerning employment and other adult activities as well likewise have had considerable influence on the increased demand for education by today's youth.

From the many discussions in newspapers and magazines, on television and radio, and with parents and youth groups, it may appear that young adolescents have not responded well to the demand for more education. The opposite is in fact true. Attendance at summer school, which is usually voluntary, and the attitudes of young adolescents toward school give some indication of youth's response to the demand for more education. In more than 75 per cent of the junior high schools in the United States, summer schools are offered for young adolescents. In a third of these schools, attendance at summer sessions has shown a marked and steady increase in recent years.

The attitudes of junior high school youth concerning their work in school likewise seem to be improving. In the survey of junior high school principals, more than two-thirds reported better attitudes of pupils toward school in the last ten years, while less than 10 per cent of the principals felt that attitudes among pupils are poorer. The cooperation of parents in the counseling problems of their children is likewise better, according to 60 per cent of the principals.

The increased continuation of youth in school into the older adolescent years is another indication of the favorable response to the demand for more education. From 1947 to 1961, the percentage of 16- and 17-year-old youths enrolled in school steadily increased, from 67.6 per cent to 83.6 per cent of those in this age group.[4] The

retention of pupils until graduation from high school likewise has steadily increased since 1948, with 710 of 1,000 pupils who entered the 5th grade in the fall of 1957 graduating in 1965.[5] The response of young adolescents to the demand for more education is, therefore, expressed through better attitudes toward school, attendance at summer school, and continuation of their education into older adolescent years.

Pressures for Academic Success

One of the most interesting developments in the American culture of the past decade has been the tremendous pressure on youth for higher achievement in academic studies. This is not unrelated to the demand for more education, and yet it has developed somewhat independently of it. Soon after World War II there was severe criticism of secondary education, especially as this was reflected in the academic studies and achievement of secondary-school youth. The criticism of secondary education reached a climax after 1957 when the Russians placed the first satellite in orbit. Little criticism was directed at the colleges and universities; the secondary school received the full attention of those who placed the blame for the great achievement of the Russians on our system of public education.

At about the same time, the population explosion of World War II began to reach the colleges, with college admissions for the first time presenting a serious problem to well-qualified youth. The college admissions problem was further intensified by the rapid increase in demands for higher education from a larger segment of our total population. Especially at the private institutions, where the high costs discouraged the number of applicants in the past, the demands for admission from highly-qualified students have far exceeded the places that were available for new students. As it became more difficult to gain admission to some institutions, the prestige associated with acceptance placed further pressures on the ambitions of students and their parents.

In the junior high school, the first response to the pressure for improved academic studies was the rapid introduction of special courses and programs for the more able pupils. Usually called "honors classes," they provided either acceleration

---

[4] National Education Association, Research Division, *NEA Research Memo,* April, 1963. Washington: National Education Association.

[5] United States Office of Education, *Digest of Educational Statistics,* 1965 Edition. Washington: Superintendent of Documents, Government Printing Office, 1965, p. 124.

or enrichment for the most able pupils in certain subject areas. On the whole the response to these programs by pupils, teachers, and parents has been exceedingly favorable. For some pupils, however, the quantity of work and the pressure for achievement in these programs has indeed been excessive. Frequently, the amount of work demanded of pupils has been greatly increased, without sufficient regard for the health and recreational needs of young adolescents. Teachers inexperienced with honors classes often find it difficult to create challenging work rather than just an increased amount of work for students. Motivation for achievement in the academic studies by young adolescents, who have great interest in creative activities, sometimes has been dulled by the demands of the honors programs. In fact, 50 per cent of the principals in the study to which reference has previously been made indicated that honors programs have created too much pressure for academic achievement for some pupils. This does not mean that they consider the response of pupils to honors programs on the whole as an unfavorable one. In fact, according to the principals, the opposite is true. It does mean, however, that the demands of honors programs on the time and energy of young adolescents has not always been in harmony with their interest in creative activities nor with their normal needs for rest, relaxation, and recreation.

Until a decade or so ago college admission was considered to be a problem primarily for the senior high school. With the increasing difficulty that attends admission to college today, the concern of pupils and their parents for college admission extends well into the junior high school grades. In fact, two-thirds of the principals indicated that early choice of college is a more serious concern of pupils in the junior high school today than a decade ago.

Early expressions of interest by young adolescents in continuing their education into the college and university are certainly desirable. Such interest can provide considerable motivation for higher achievement in the junior high school, may help in the better choice of elective studies and activities, and should prevent a mad rush by pupils in the senior high school to identify appropriate colleges. At the same time, the early choice of a specific college or university may lead to unnecessary frustration and disappointment when pupils and parents learn later that such early choices were not realistic for the abilities of the pupils or the financial means of the parents.

Early interest in post-secondary education and in certain types of educational institutions may indeed be appropriate for young adolescents. The choice of specific institutions should be delayed, however, until counselors, pupils, and parents can evaluate in proper perspective the abilities, academic motivations, personal qualities, and family backgrounds that may bear on admission to and success in post-secondary schools. The current response of young adolescents to the pressures of academic studies and higher academic achievement, although favorable in many respects, presents unique problems to those responsible for guidance and counseling in the junior high school.

Social Sophistication in Our Society

The affluence of people in America has no doubt been a major factor in the rapid spread of sophisticated social activities and relationships to a larger segment of our total population. The automobile, television, vacation travel, and better personal dress and appearance are now available to almost every employed person and his family. With these have come sophistication in our social life which would have been impossible a generation ago.

For adults much of the sophistication that we see may be considered wholesome and desirable. Among young adolescents, however, the response to the sophistication in our society is frequently excessive and inappropriate, if not actually harmful. For instance, a high percentage of principals report that, as compared with a decade ago, they have a greater problem with extreme hairdos and make-up by girls, smoking by both boys and girls, and late parties for youth in homes and community centers. Some of the principals (28 per cent) also stated that drinking has become an increasing problem among young adolescents. In a few communities (16 per cent) party crashing has likewise become a problem, although apparently not as serious as among older adolescents. The fact that some of these problems are reported by a minority of the principals should not detract from their seriousness. If they occur at all among substantial numbers of young adolescents it should be of concern to educators and parents.

The interest of young adolescents in improving their personal appearance and in wholesome social activities, however, should be commended. It is the excessive response of young adolescents to the sophistication in our culture which should cause us concern. Understanding help and supervision from parents, teachers and other adults for young adolescents in all their activities should serve to direct them toward wholesome behavior in their social growth and development.

Boy-Girl Relationships

There is little doubt that in our society there has been a tremendous change in the relationships between boys and girls as they grow from early adolescence into adulthood. The greater permissiveness granted youth by their parents and other adults is largely responsible for these changing relationships. Other factors have also influenced this development. The automobile, especially for older adolescents, has given youth freedom of movement which their elders a generation ago could not enjoy. The drive-in theater, the drive-in hot dog and hamburger stands, and, especially for older youth, the resort areas—all these are a prominent part of our adolescent culture in America today. Early marriage, once limited to out-of-school youth, is increasing among youth still in high school, and many college undergraduates are married, frequently in their freshman or sophomore year.

Although these developments in our adolescent culture apply primarily to older youth, they are also reflected in the boy-girl relationships among young adolescents. For instance, there is earlier steady dating among young adolescents, 60 per cent of the principals reporting that this problem is more serious than a decade ago. Perhaps even more serious is the dating of young adolescent girls by older boys, considered to be a serious problem by 47 per cent of the principals. A generation ago a senior high school boy was rarely seen with a junior high school girl as his date. Today the older boy with a driver's license, his own jalopy or the family car, and spending money is indeed attractive to girls several years younger, while the mature-appearing girl, with the help of sophisticated hairdos, make-up, and dress is of interest to older boys. Consequently, we have today dating relationships between boys and girls which confound their teachers and worry their parents. Although we may not be happy about it, the changing relationships of boys and girls is a response, even as young adolescents, to the culture of today.

Summary

The response of young adolescents to present-day culture is therefore a varied one, in some respects favorable and wholesome, in others unfavorable, improper, or inappropriate. The urbanization of our society—the most dominant influence on our culture today—has brought greater mobility in our population, instability in home and family life, and lack of unity in our urban communities. Especially in urban areas, sharply increased juvenile delinquency among young adolescents has been the result. Tensions between ethnic groups, although apparently increasing among young adolescents, have not been as serious as those tensions have been among adults.

The greater social sophistication in our adult culture likewise has been reflected in the attitudes and conduct of young adolescents. There has been much change among young adolescents, especially in boy-girl relationships, seen in earlier steady dating and more dating of young adolescent girls and older boys. There has likewise been acceleration among young adolescents in such expressions of sophistication as smoking, use of make-up, hairdos, hours for social activities, and, in some communities, drinking.

The most favorable response of young adolescents to our present-day culture has been toward the demand for more education. Their attitudes toward school are better, they take more advantage of educational opportunities for young adolescents, and increasing numbers continue in school beyond the compulsory attendance years. Even the pressures for academic achievement, although they may be unduly severe for some youth, have brought a favorable response from young adolescents as a whole.

The response of young adolescents to present-day culture demands continuous study and evaluation by parents, educators, and other citizens, who should give direction to the program of the school, improve understanding between parents and youth, and identify more fully the place of young adolescents in the life of the community.

Chapter 2

The Influence of Present-Day Culture on the Functions of the Junior High School

Mauritz Johnson, Jr.
Professor of Secondary Education
Cornell University

It is an interesting paradox that in the American educational tradition the schools reflect the contemporary culture. Eloquent arguments have been put forth to support the contention that education —true education—is universally the same regardless of time or place. But whatever education ought to be, the fact remains that the schools of this country have always been responsive to societal needs and cultural changes, insofar as these needs and changes have been correctly interpreted.

This is not to say that the purposes and programs of schools are in a constant state of flux or upheaval. Indeed, one of the needs of every society is the selective transmission of its cultural heritage. Every curriculum is the result of deliberate selections from the transmissible cultural content. These selections are made in accordance with societal values and imperatives. As social institutions, schools reflect in their forms and goals both the enduring traditions and the current temper of the society which establishes and sustains them. Education must have both a timeless and a timely quality.

The persistence of anachronistic institutional forms and goals tends to inhibit social progress and to invite societal dislocations. These effects are minimized when institutions evolve in response to cultural change through a process of innovation and adaptation and a critical re-examination of tradition. Under conditions of precipitous cultural change, yesterday's innovations become today's traditions, themselves subject to review in the light of altered realities.

The Junior High School as a Reflection of the Culture

The junior high school has undergone some evolution since its inception, but many features which have already become traditional stand in need of review. This institution emerged as a distinct organizational unit as a result of the deliberations and recommendations of some half-dozen national committees which met during the quarter century beginning in 1892. The four-year public high school had scarcely supplanted the semi-private academy and been grafted to the eight-grade common school system when agitation began for the reorganization of secondary education into a six-year format. By 1920 a number of books on the junior high school had appeared, and a full-fledged movement was under way.

Although every junior high school that was ever established was rationalized on educational grounds, many apparently were organized for reasons of local expediency. Even the rational arguments put forth for the junior high school were so diverse and, if not actually contradictory, so unrelated as to appear more often to justify what was desired than what was desirable.

There was, in the first place, the matter of economy of time, sought by President Eliot of Harvard to shorten the college preparatory period. This goal was never actually achieved, although preparation for college may well have been strengthened through the implementation by the junior high school of the Committee of Ten's recommendations for the earlier introduction, of academic studies. Yet, it was not with the college-bound group that the early junior high schools were chiefly concerned, but rather with the terminal students, the "laggards in our schools," who as a result of the continual extension and more effective enforcement of compulsory education laws were required to remain in school longer and whose parents, with the closing of the frontier, increasingly found in schooling the only avenue to economic opportunity and social mobility open to their children.

In a period of unprecedented immigration, growing industrialization and increasing urbanization, various elements in the society promoted a vocationalization of the American schools. The establishment of junior high schools created an opportunity to provide vocational programs to a larger number of pupils at an earlier age. Vocational guidance was a logical accompaniment, and with the increasing diversity of programs and the attendant enlargement of choice, educational guidance became a virtual necessity.

Developments in psychology during the first decade of the century added support for the junior high school idea. Studies of adolescence emphasized that for many individuals puberty coincided more nearly with seventh grade than with the first year of the four-year high school. The development of standardized tests of intelligence and achievement emphasized extensive individual differences, and this was taken to suggest a need for greater diversity in the educational program than the existing elementary school afforded its older pupils. The rejection of faculty psychology and its correlative notion of transfer of learning through mental discipline not only gave sanction to the emphasis on vocational training but led also to a pressure for similar direct training for citizenship duties, family responsibilities, and leisure activities, through a "practical" program of "life-like" learning activities.

At about this time, the pragmatic American outlook which had found expression in the philosophy of Pierce and James was further refined as the scientific-democratic experimentalism of John Dewey. World War I dealt tradition a heavy blow. Cherished assumptions were in general strained if not shattered, and more specifically, the physical and emotional fitness of conscripts was found wanting, trained manpower was needed for industrial and agricultural production, and a new concept of responsible citizenship appropriate for a new world power emerged. The "cardinal principles" report of 1918 promulgated a list of objectives which made the secondary school responsible for direct preparation for citizenship and social efficiency. Recognizing that science and democracy had become the dominant cultural themes, Dewey enunciated a theory of education stressing direct experience, scientific method, and social values.

When direct preparation for personal living and civic participation became the chief objectives of schools, it appeared to some more logical to organize learning experiences in terms of societal problems and the persistent life functions of all individuals than on the basis of academic subjects derived from disciplines structured to exemplify meaningful relationships among ideas. If subjects were retained, their content was viewed primarily as data to be applied to specific problems, rather than as a body of significant concepts and principles, derived through accepted methods of inquiry and ordered to facilitate the development of a serviceable cognitive structure. Indeed, for most students, intellectual development was considered an unrealistic goal, and for the few who planned on further education, mastery of academic subjects was considered necessary only to meet the irrational requirements of colleges and universities.

Thus, the junior high school developed during a period when the cultural demands upon the schools were interpreted as calling for an emphasis upon the development of social efficiency, construed as the ability to cope effectively with personal problems and to cooperate with others in the solution of societal problems. If the schools dared not build a new social order, they did undertake to equip students to adjust to life as they found it and to recognize the shortcomings of the existing social order. The social studies, still grappling with the difficult problems of combining humanistic history with a coterie of social sciences, became primarily concerned with citizenship and social adjustment and served as the focus of all general education. Committed to such process goals as democratic classroom living and scientific group problem solving, the social studies became the epitome of the junior high school.

Re-examination of the Culture and the Junior High School

A reassessment of the posture which the schools had assumed, ostensibly in response to cultural forces and societal demands, was under way in the late 1950's when, a mere 12 years after the dawn of the atomic age, the era of space exploration began. Amid undertones of apprehension and competitiveness in a Cold War setting, the fundamental realizations that slowly emerged were that a society's strength and progress depend on individual excellence and that the significant accomplishments and challenging frontiers in the further evolution of mankind would lie in the intellectual realm. If the schools were not to be completely out of tune with the advancing culture, they would have to recognize and affirm as their primary responsibility the intellectual development of all pupils within a climate of striving by each for excellence in various endeavors.

Accepted functions of the junior high school such as integration, socialization, articulation, differentiation, and exploration and guidance were not invalidated, but they clearly had to be subordinated and re-interpreted. It was necessary to recognize that some functions were not relevant to the formal curriculum, but rather were met in the total setting of the school and, indeed, in the very existence of a comprehensive secondary school. The accepted functions represented a mixture of instrumental conditions, desirable by-products, and subsidiary goals of the junior high school. The school's primary objectives have at best been implied and at worst ignored, and the times call for their explication and reaffirmation.

The cultural progress which for a period had been sustained by inventive technicians, skilled artisans, and resourceful entrepreneurs has come increasingly to depend upon highly specialized theoretical knowledge. The foundation of an advanced society is its intellectual resources. These resources must be deliberately and assiduously cultivated, and the primary responsibility for their cultivation falls upon the schools at all levels. The acquisition of basic knowledge and significant ideas, the development of an efficacious cognitive structure, the cultivation of skills and habits of inquiry and thought, and the nourishing of intellectual interests require long, sustained effort and must, therefore, begin early. Representing as they do a period of personal transition, the junior high school years may well be crucial ones in determining whether the process of intellectual growth loses impetus or is sustained and accelerated.

Technological progress depends upon scientific advances, and both require specialization. It is not only for the benefit of future specialists, however, that increased intellectual emphasis is necessary in the schools. All who are to live and participate intelligently in a culture dominated by science need to achieve scientific and mathematical literacy, if not sophistication. Otherwise they will be aliens in their own society. Furthermore, they will be incapable, as citizens, of understanding the issues on which they will be asked to take stands and they will increasingly face the risk of having to forfeit their policy-making right to technical experts. As the social sciences acquire increased precision in predicting individual behavior and social phenomena, a systematic understanding of them also becomes increasingly important for any educated person.

But significant as the natural sciences are as the hallmarks of contemporary culture, and as instrumental as the social sciences may be destined to become in the achievement of "the great society," they only serve to make possible a fuller life, and the crucial question is, "With what will that life be filled?" That it will be filled increasingly with leisure hours seems certain. What new opportunities will be created for the use of leisure time it is impossible even to surmise. Surely, however, the heritage of ideas, values, and artistic creations from mankind's past will continue to be a source of delight to man. But, if a wider segment of the populace is to find meaning in life in the midst of dizzying change, the schools must give greater attention to the cultivation of intellectual interests and aesthetic sensitivity.

What the present-day culture suggests for the junior high school, then, is an increased emphasis upon intellectual development, not only to produce the brainpower upon which cultural progress depends, but also to enable all individuals to participate fully in their culture, and, indeed, to equip them to take advantage of whatever vocational training and re-training they may find they need. It is essential that the schools not discount the intellectual potentials of students by devising inferior substitute programs of an apparently more practical nature. When nothing is so certain as change, both in the students' own development and in the culture in which they live, it is unwise for the school to be overly preoccupied with adolescence on the one hand or with explicit vocational and citizenship training on the other.

Chapter 3

Planning Curriculum Programs for Young Adolescents

John H. Lounsbury
Chairman of Department of Education
Georgia College at Milledgeville

Whether by evolution or revolution, the social studies curriculum needs drastic overhauling. It is provincial, out-dated, and sterile. Such statements could have been made 40 years ago—and were. Likewise, they could be made today—and are!

That the curriculum in American education lags behind current needs and demands is well known and frequently documented. Forty-one years ago Rugg stated, "Not once in a century and a half of national history has the curriculum of the school caught up with the dynamic content of American life."[1] The intervening years have not altered the basic validity of this statement, though innumerable curriculum improvement programs, projects, and proposals of every conceivable hue and variety have been carried out. The bulk of these programs have failed to make any enduring difference, partly because they were based on false assumptions about the nature of curriculum change. Rugg's evaluation of the situation, made in the same writing quoted above, continues sound:

Partial, superficial, and timorous "revision" rather than general, fundamental, and courageous reconstruction characterizes curriculum-making in the public schools . . . the existing program is always taken as a point of departure . . . Thus curriculum-making becomes a process of accretion and elimination. There is little, indeed almost no movement under way in public schools to initiate curriculum-making from the starting point either of child learning or of the institutions and problems of American life. For over fifty years, tinkering has characterized the attack on the curriculum.[2]

What is true generally of the school curriculum is no less true of the social studies. Certainly social studies educators have not distinguished themselves as curriculum innovators.[3] Some of the more comprehensive changes that have been made in social studies education are not viewed universally as representing progress.[4] Defenders of current practices in social studies education, however, no matter what their philosophical persuasions, are conspicuous by their absence. There is, then, work to be done.

The crux of the junior high school curriculum problem can be stated succinctly as follows: The junior high school curriculum is essentially a common, general education program, but it is offered to students who are distinguished by the degree to which they differ from one another. Or to put it another way, at no other level are the individual differences greater while the program is so similar. At the elementary school level a variety of sub-groups, reading groups, interest groups, and the like are utilized with varied texts to accommodate individual differences within the

---

[2] *Ibid.*, p. 427.

[3] For a current and notable exception see Harold M. Long and Robert N. King, *Improving the Teaching of World Affairs: The Glens Falls Story*, Bulletin No. 35. Washington: National Council for the Social Studies, NEA, 1964.

[4] See, for example, Charles R. Keller, "Needed: A Revolution in the Social Studies," *Saturday Review*, September 16, 1961.

---

[1] Rugg, Harold, *Curriculum-Making: Past and Present,* Twenty-Sixth Yearbook of N.S.S.E., Part I, 1926, p. 3.

self-contained classroom. At the senior high school level, by the elective program, varied curricular tracks, and unfortunately by dropping out, individual differences are recognized and accommodated. But at the junior high school level, different as pupils are, they all tend to take the same program.

Individual Differences and the Curriculum

The facts concerning individual differences are probably the most important factor underlying any attempt to provide comprehensive educational experiences for young people. The complete unanimity and similarity of pupils may be a utopian concept for teachers to contemplate in moments of despair. The simplicity and efficiency of education, were such a unanimity to be true, might be a wonder to behold. How easy it would be to teach. How simple it would be to administer. Yet, one does not have to dwell long on such a reverie to realize how undesirable and stultifying, how unexciting, such a condition would be. Even the most tired teachers on Friday afternoon would quickly reject such an apparently utopian concept, for individual differences, although at times a seeming burden to teachers, are the realities which give real meaning and significance to all education and to every teacher's efforts.

In the full light of individual differences, efforts at curriculum planning are *partially* defeated even before they start. As Wilhelms has pointed out, "Curriculums are planned for groups rather than for individuals, and that fact may as well be recognized at the outset."[5] A recognition of this truth clearly brings to the forefront the inevitable and, in some respects, unsolvable problem that curriculum development must deal with. From such a standpoint, it must be acknowledged that curriculum planning can never be *fully* effective. It must always involve, to some degree, generalizations based on hunches, best bets, and hopes, to be taken with a grain of salt, for any time that adults make plans for a group of children when those children are not known as individuals, some clear violation of individual interests and needs will inevitably result. Yet plans must be made, a curriculum must be organized, for school systems that encompass more than a fourth of a nation cannot operate without considerable planning and policy.

Teachers must understand why plans and guides have been prepared by various officials, yet recognize why these materials are in some ways inappropriate for their particular group at some particular time. They should be ready, willing, and able to use materials as springboards for providing the experiences that come from their own unique understanding of the youngsters, and not reluctantly accept plans and guides as dictums from "on high" that must be followed. No schoolwide or system-wide plan of grouping or curriculum organization can make the specific provisions that need to be made. In the final analysis the classroom teacher is the only one that can provide for individual differences. All that can be done by a state department, a particular school system's curriculum committee, or, even an individual school's faculty, is to provide guidelines, suggestions, and broad outlines. The production of such guidelines or bulletins may often appear to be the major curriculum development effort, but this is really only preliminary to the main show, the show that begins when the classroom teacher starts to interact with her students. At this point the teacher has amazingly complete and full responsibility to determine what is taught and how it is taught. Existing curriculum guides and materials may be used, or they may just as easily be by-passed. An immediate student interest may be developed or overlooked; it all depends on the judgment of the classroom teacher. Is it any wonder, when he considered the breadth of responsibility which our American system of education gives to the individual classroom teacher, that Archibald McLeish referred to "the terrible responsibility" of the teacher? Surely fully professional teachers need to be in every classroom to carry out the American approach to education.

Curriculum development for young adolescents must be viewed in the context described above. Yet how logical and easy it is to make assumptions about the difference that can be made by changing curriculum materials and planning new programs on paper. It is because of just such assumptions that many well-intended programs never achieved anticipated significance. Curriculum development programs, if they are to contribute to the pupils' learnings, must be built on a clear understanding that the classroom teacher is the agent of curriculum change. All curriculum development efforts essentially are in-service education efforts directed toward making more able and professional teachers. These efforts should seek to improve individuals, to make it possible

5 Wilhelms, Fred T., "The Curriculum and Individual Differences," *Individualizing Instruction, Sixty-first NSSE Yearbook,* Part I, 1962, p. 62.

for teachers to make more effective curriculum decisions as they interact with boys and girls. Any other approach to curriculum development is likely to lead up a blind alley. Too often our best laid plans and exciting new guides, although sincerely and conscientiously developed by groups, have had little or no effect on the actual learning experiences of young people during school. Kimball Wiles clearly stated this reality of curriculum planning when he wrote, "The real curriculum is the one the pupil experiences. Actually the expectations of curriculum designers may be illusions and the teacher's guides and syllabi mere paper representations of hollow hopes."[6] Educators must recognize and conscientiously take into account the enduring significance of the classroom teacher as the agent of curriculum change. This concept, of course, is not a new one. Alice Miel discussed it many years ago in her important little volume, *Changing the Curriculum*, in which she developed the position that changing the curriculum means changing people.[7]

The Individual Curriculum

Teachers err by continuing to assume falsely that they "teach" a class, and they plan their lessons accordingly. Yet it is obvious that one really cannot teach a class at all, for a class has no mind; it is simply an administratively established grouping of individuals, each of whom learns as an individual. What the individual pupils learn is varied. They do not learn what the teacher teaches; some learn one thing and some learn another from the same teacher effort and instruction. There is in fact not "a" curriculum, but there are as many curricula as there are individual pupils in a class. The curriculum for each individual pupil is made up of those learnings which he selects, accepts, and incorporates into himself. Many teachers would undoubtedly be surprised to see the degree to which the real curriculum of individual pupils differs from one student to another, although all these students sit side by side in the same classroom.

The disparity between what is learned from common experiences is a source of amazement

and frustration to teachers, mainly because they insist on holding unrealistic common standards and expectations for all pupils. From the very moment a teacher starts teaching something to a class he needs to realize that some pupils *already* know more about the topic than some others will *after* several days of "teaching."

Comprehensive Curriculum Planning

To emphasize the crucial importance of the individual teacher in the individual classroom is not to imply that curriculum planning should and can be done solely by individual teachers within actual classroom situations, for such a view is neither correct nor sound. Curriculum planning should be done by faculties, school systems, state departments, and others who have leadership responsibilities as well as the administrative resources. In addition, the students and parents have a major stake in curriculum planning and should be actively involved. Curriculum work on levels above the classroom level, however, should be done with the clear recognition that the plans will be implemented by individual teachers if they are to be implemented at all. Much of the foundational and preliminary aspects of curriculum planning must, of course, be done on a level above the classroom. In fact, there is little reason to believe that an individual teacher will be an active agent of positive curriculum change except as he is motivated, directed, and supported by plans and projects involving other professional personnel.

A good beginning point for curriculum planning efforts is in the basic area of purposes. There simply is no effective shortcut that bypasses good hard thinking about the objectives of education, particularly social studies objectives. Teachers tend to ignore, such considerations, feeling that this is something done in college education classes but that it has little to do with the day-in and day-out instruction of a group of adolescents. Yet, every decision made by the teacher regarding what he teaches and how he teaches it reflects his conscious or subconscious set of educational objectives and his value commitments. Curriculum planning involves making choices, and making choices necessarily involves objectives and values. Those who would effectively work in curriculum planning as individuals or as part of a professional team must know clearly what they believe in and what ends they seek to achieve. Only as a particular goal is in mind can it be determined whether one subject is better than another, or one curricu-

[6] Kimball Wiles in the Foreword to *The Junior High School We Saw*, by John H. Lounsbury and Jean V. Marani, The Association for Supervision and Curriculum Development, National Education Association, 1964, p. v.

[7] Alice Miel, *Changing the Curriculum: A Social Process*, New York: D. Appleton-Century Co., Inc., 1946.

lum organization proposal is superior to another. After all, if you do not know where you are going, any road will lead there.

Social studies teachers, probably more than other teachers, have been guilty of making blithe assumptions about the understanding of social studies objectives. They sometimes tend to feel righteous, because their courses are universally required by state departments, local boards, and other duly constituted bodies of officials. Because social studies courses are always required, the objectives must be commonly known and self-evident, they reason. Yet the fact of the matter is that one of the major reasons why social studies instruction consistently is rated low by pupils, especially drop-outs, is that they do not see any significance in the study of social studies. Young people who complain of being tired in connection with their school work often are really questioning the value of their assignments rather than stating a fact of their physical condition.

Junior high school students, perhaps even more so than other students, are characterized by curiosity and are concerned with the world about them. They are concerned with the world that they are now beginning to analyze and evaluate, the world on which they will live. The past seems to hold relatively little interest for them except as its relationship to the present has been made clear. This means that the teacher must be especially aware of the correlations between the past and the present in social studies instruction.

Teachers might deny the narrowness of their objectives, but a survey of existing practices and a careful analysis of their examinations would readily reveal—and indeed surveys have done just so—that the overarching objective of social studies instruction, *as actually carried out*, is the mastery of content presented in text and lecture. "Filling little mugs from teacher's jug," describes an older view of teaching that would be rejected verbally by most teachers, but nevertheless endorsed by their practices.

Teachers really concerned with curriculum planning must therefore contemplate seriously and deeply what their purposes are in each of the courses they teach. Only as a teacher clarifies these purposes can he communicate them to students. And only as the students see his purposes can they even accept them, let alone alter them or make them their own.

A consideration of the objectives of social studies should immediately make clear the broad responsibilities which rest with instructors in this field. No other single subject area has at least a partial responsibility for so many of the generally accepted objectives of education. A study of the Seven Cardinal Principles (objectives) or the Ten Imperative Needs of Youth will quickly show that practically all of these commonly accepted objectives are, in part, the responsibility of social studies teachers. In addition, such a thoughtful consideration of these lists of objectives would also reveal the striking fact that none of them *necessarily* requires full mastery or coverage of the chronological development of either world or American history. Social studies objectives, unlike its content, tend to lie in the future rather than in the past. They deal predominantly with attitudes and social studies skills that carry over into adult life, such as cartoon analysis, ability to read and interpret graphs, ability to distinguish between fact and opinion, and the ability to organize information for effective presentation either orally or in writing. These objectives must be a prime order of business, not hoped-for by-products of a mad rush through the annals of the history of man. As consideration is given to objectives, all of the generally accepted foundations of curriculum development will become involved, as they should. Decisions about educational practices should not be made apart from beliefs about how we learn, democratic principles, and the social realities of our day. Indeed these factors are the proper determinants of curriculum decisions and any plans which fail to recognize their rightful influence are doomed to fail in the long run.

Because, in the final analysis, the curriculum is really made in the classroom, it should be readily apparent why so much careful planning done by others at higher levels never pays off even though it is based on a consideration of the foundations. If those who control the minute-by-minute curriculum decisions are not of the same mind, do not hold the same values, do not seek to achieve the same objectives as those who planned the course of study, wrote the textbook, or who otherwise preplanned the curriculum, the efforts of the latter group can readily be ignored or contradicted. The values and the objectives of the individual teacher are what must be altered if you would change the curriculum. Fox has developed such a position in an article which included the chart reproduced as Figure 1. This diagram shows the relationship of values and objectives to the final curriculum.

FIGURE 1

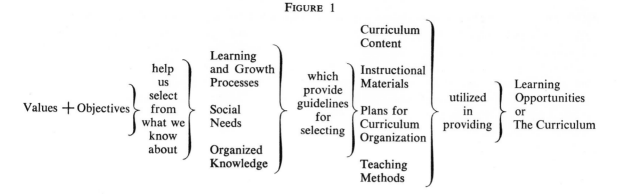

Fox explains the importance of the values (Figure 1) of the teacher as follows:

Participants in the curriculum improvement process may make use of what is known about effective motivation of the learner if it fits the values they are trying to implement. Otherwise they will select other, less effective ways to motivate. For example, if it is known that if a child is engaged in solving a problem that is real to him, his motivation is high and his learning efficient. If we deem it important for a child to learn something which does not make sense to him, we may "require" it, or grade him on it, or tell him that it is good for him. Similarly, the person interested in promoting "transference of the cultural heritage" may give close attention to research on the most efficient ways of committing a body of knowledge to memory, overlooking the research on rate of forgetting. The person who puts a high value on an intensively nationalistic kind of patriotism places considerable emphasis on knowing the rules for displaying the American flag, but overlooks the importance of young people being familiar with the functions and activities of the United Nations Security Council.

Not only do one's values influence the choice of basic principles of guidelines, but they are involved at the level of implementation. Decisions regarding teaching methods, the design of learning experiences, or instructional materials, can be and are circumvented by the classroom teacher who finds his own values and objectives inconsistent with these resources. Since "curriculum" ultimately consist of the actual learning experiences in which the pupils are engaged, the classroom teacher has the "last word,"

and his values may prove to be the most influential of all.[8]

Conclusion

Curriculum planning for young adolescents is a vital job, a job calling for experts, for the help of administrators, supervisors, and specialists, but a job primarily of the individual classroom teacher. For the teacher, curriculum planning is simply good teaching, teaching with an awareness of the full import and obligations of this demanding professional task. It is a task that puts the person of the teacher front and center, for what is taught and how it is taught tend to pale in significance when compared with who teaches. In the final analysis, there is only one thing a teacher can be sure he teaches to all his pupils—himself.

To be sure, the problems faced by teachers are manifold, the rationalizations for doing nothing are abundant and readily acceptable to others, the physical limitations and handicaps to more effective instruction are painfully apparent. Yet, the call to improve instruction is clarion and the responsibility of the professional teacher is unavoidable. There is no situation so restricting, so impossible, but that it could not be significantly improved if the teacher concerned willed it.

[8] Fox, Robert S., "Curriculum Development With a Purpose," *Theory Into Practice*, October, 1962, p. 204.

Section II

Sample Programs of Social Studies Instruction

In Section One attention has been given to the cultural impact on the junior high school and upon the young adolescent. In recognition of this cultural influence, consideration of the problem of curriculum design for the junior high school points out some qualities deemed essential in programs for young adolescents.

To illustrate curriculum patterns in junior high school, a number of schools across the nation have given descriptions of their social studies offerings. Section Two includes general descriptions of programs from five schools, usually confined for illustrative purposes to descriptions of one grade. One program is included for its innovative value in that it represents the non-graded school organization.

The reader will be aware of the concern for individual differences expressed in these selected programs. The variation regarding the stated purpose of the junior high school represented among the schools probably indicates the present uncertainty regarding curriculum content for this age level. At this time of considerable experimentation and research in curriculum improvement, it might have been supposed that more programs would conduct such investigation. The programs presented in this section range from somewhat traditional and conservative organizations to those in which more liberal and flexible philosophies prevail. From these varied approaches suggestions for experimentation may be derived. These programs are presented not necessarily as examples to be imitated but as representative of junior high school programs of today in terms of traditional organization with some evidence of experimentation.

Chapter 4

The Vancouver, Washington, Social Studies Program

McLoughlin Junior High School
Emphasis on Grade 9

Emily Hudgin
Secondary Consultant in Social Studies and English
Vancouver Public Schools
Vancouver, Washington
and
W. Ford Hoke
Principal of McLoughlin Junior High School
Vancouver, Washington

In this world, with its ever increasing changes in knowledge and technology, the Vancouver curriculum directors have been increasingly aware of the necessity for upgrading and revising the social studies curriculum from kindergarten through the 12th grade in the Vancouver Public Schools. The revisions were based upon the philosophy of the school system and, more specifically, the philosophy as related to the junior high school.

Philosophy of the School System

The social studies are planned experiences and activities arranged to help students understand and appreciate their cultural heritage and man's reaction to his changing environment. Through the social studies, students are helped to understand themselves and others; to learn to adjust to changing conditions; to develop positive attitudes and values; to develop critical thinking; and to develop resourceful and intelligent behavior—thus building the academic and social competencies and skills needed for responsible democratic citizenship.

Students, through the study of meaningful problems, are helped to relate their observations and discoveries to all of the social and natural sciences. Students will focus attention on finding out how people live in the community, state, nation, and the world. They will become familiar with the contribution of the past to the present, and will learn that men must cooperate to live together.

The curriculum is planned so that learning activity for every student is provided. The social studies are all-encompassing and thus play a vital role in the total development of each student.[1]

Philosophy of the Junior High School

The philosophy of the junior high school follows the basic school philosophy. The program of the junior high school is planned around the fact that this age is a transitional time in a young person's life. It is manifestly true that coping with individual differences is never more important than during this stage of development.

Teachers need to use tact, patience, understanding, appreciation, and a variety of techniques so that every ability may be challenged and attracted. Principals, deans, counsellors, and instructional

---

[1] Department of Social Studies, Vancouver Public Schools. *A Guide for the Teaching of Social Studies in the Ninth Grade of the Vancouver, Washington, Public Schools.* Vancouver: Board of Education, 1963, p. i.

consultants aid the teachers in providing education for every adolescent to the optimum of his ability.[2]

The Approach

In the spring of 1960, Superintendent R. C. Bates launched a program of meetings with teacher groups to discuss areas of curricular concern. One of the findings was that teachers were becoming increasingly dissatisfied with some segments of the social studies program. A plan was then set in motion which would completely evaluate present offerings and lay the groundwork for reorganization and improvement.

During the summer of 1960, preliminary research was accomplished by a committee. This committee compiled a handbook which outlined the present program, indicated problem areas, and suggested a plan for implementing a complete study of the total social studies curriculum.

In the fall of 1960, a full-scale project was launched to evaluate, revise, and update the social studies curriculum. Chairmen were selected from each grade level and organized into a "steering committee." This group of leaders met with Dr. Ray Jongeward, Director of Instruction, and Dr. Clifford Foster of the University of Washington. Dr. Foster, as a consultant, helped to organize and guide the study.

Following preliminary planning by the steering committee, grade-level chairmen met with fellow teachers at grade-level meetings. At each grade level meeting, units taught, concepts developed, and skills implemented for particular areas in the social studies were listed. At various times the steering committee met to evaluate progress and make future plans. An all-district social studies teachers' meeting was held to keep everyone informed of progress being made and future plans and organization.

In May 1961, a summer study of the social studies was authorized under the supervision of Dr. Jongeward, and teachers from each grade level were hired to move the project along as far as time would allow. Specifically, the summer research called for a statement of philosophy of the social studies and the list of objectives that would encompass all levels from kindergarten through grade 12. Each grade level also was to develop a resource unit built around one of the themes for that level. These resource units were then to

be made available for each social studies teacher in the fall. These units included the title, specific objectives to be accomplished for that unit, concepts, pupil experiences, and a bibliography. Dr. Foster was available for further consultation.

A continuation of the study followed during the 1961–1962 school year. Each resource unit that had been developed was used and critically analyzed. Teachers completed and shared other resource units on their grade level. These were compiled and made available for all teachers and also were made readily available to lay people and all others interested or concerned.

The 1961–1962 school year was a year of transition and exploration. During the following year the district completely revised the social studies curriculum, purchased new up-to-date materials, and completed guidebooks stating in detail the new course of study from K–12.

A Continuing Evaluation of the Program

In the adoption of this series of guides it is noted that curriculum content in our troubled times is subject to constant re-evaluation and revision. This concept of fluid evolution is notably pertinent to the field of social studies. It is planned that a continuing committee of teachers will reassess this program annually and prepare supplements to these guides as new information and circumstances may require.

This project of revising the social studies program is part of a pervasive program of curriculum revision in this school district. Other areas of the curriculum have been re-evaluated during the past three years and still others are currently subject to re-examination. Curriculum development today must necessarily be a very dynamic process. We take much pride in the advanced character of Vancouver's educational program. There is no one area of our total endeavor where this character is more revealing than in the attention currently given to curriculum revision.

Successful and significant curriculum revision is always an effort of informed and highly motivated teachers. This series of guides is basically a teacher effort. Many of our most distinguished teachers have contributed to this effort. The success of the undertaking is basically a credit to them. We would like to note, however, that advice and counsel has been given by leaders of our instructional staff and by a number of consultants who came to Vancouver to assist in the effort. Dr. Clifford Foster of the University of Washington

---

[2] Information supplied by W. Ford Hoke, Principal, McLoughlin Junior High School, Vancouver, Washington.

has offered guiding influence as prime consultant since the inception of the program. Dr. Ray Jongeward was the initiator of the project at the time that he served as Director of Instruction for the Vancouver Public Schools. Mr. Elmer Lindquist, Director of Elementary Instruction, has provided leadership for the project since Dr. Jongeward's departure.

It is necessary to emphasize that this project could not have been accomplished without the basic contributions of the many participating class-room teachers. The revised course of study cannot become effective without understanding and pur-poseful implementation by the classroom teachers for whose use this material has been prepared. In this instance, as in others, effective curriculum development depends primarily on the competence and diligence of classroom teachers.[3]

Objectives of the Social Studies Program

The social studies are all encompassing and thus play a vital role in the total development of each student.

The objectives of the social studies program seem to be best stated in the following form:

1. To develop understanding of man and society;
2. To provide experiences and build skills which will aid in the development of responsible citizenship in a democracy;
3. To develop an awareness of the nature and structure of a democratic society and the rela-tionship of each individual to it;
4. To promote respect, understanding and appre-ciation of races, religions, minorities, nations and cultures;
5. To create an awareness that man must adapt to changing conditions;
6. To provide experiences that will inspire stu-dents to think critically and make decisions on their own;
7. To develop the ability to solve effectively social problems through intelligent use of the scien-tific method;
8. To stimulate creativity, intellectual curiosity, the thrill of discovery, and an attitude of urgency toward learning;
9. To provide an understanding of moral and spiritual values and their application to every-day living;
10. To cultivate the aesthetic nature of man;
11. To develop an appreciation of our nation's political, social and cultural heritages and the historical significance of the past to the future;
12. To create an awareness of man's economic interdependence and an appreciation and un-derstanding of the free enterprise system;
13. To understand the problems which arise be-cause of growth in population, mobility of people, technological advancements, business expansion, and governmental functions;
14. To develop an awareness and understanding of the active conflict between the two major ideologies in the world today;
15. To understand the importance of our natural resources and the policies which must be ac-cepted to guarantee maximum utilization now and in the years to come; and
16. To provide experiences that will promote the development of each student to the full capa-bilities of his maximum potential.[4]

Scope and Sequence

The entire scope and sequence of the social studies has been designed around the desire to fulfill the previously stated objectives and philosophy. The success of this portion of the curriculum offer-ings to boys and girls depends on each teacher's familiarity with and understanding of the total program. It is particularly important that each teacher become cognizant of the concepts devel-oped by the preceding and following grade levels to assure the continuity of learnings within the total program.

The sequence in kindergarten through grade 7 follows the "expanding community" concept of organization. State requirements figure promi-nently in the grade 8 through 12 program. The following is the kindergarten through grade 12 social studies sequence:

Grade Level

Kindergarten	Living Together at Home and School
1	Living in Our Neighborhood
2	Living in the Community
3	Living in the Lower Columbia River Valley at Vancouver
4	Living in the State of Washington
5	Living in the United States
6	Living in the Western World
7	Living in the Eastern World
8	United States
9	Washington State History and Government and Comparative World Cultures
10	World History
11	United States History
12	Contemporary World Problems

[3] Comments by R. C. Bates, Superintendent of Schools, Vancouver, Washington.

[4] Department of Social Studies, *op. cit.*, pp. iii–iv.

Explanation of Guide

The following guides for each grade level of instruction contain the broad concepts and objectives toward which the listed learning activities and references have been directed. It is believed the concepts and objectives are important for all students to grasp. The unit outlines, time allotments, learning activities and references have been developed to assist the teacher in planning the year's activities.

The activities or experiences suggested are offered as a reservoir of ideas which may be utilized as a teacher and students work through a unit. The teacher is not expected to use all the experiences listed or to be limited to the activities mentioned. The suggested activities will need to be adapted to fit the particular teaching situation, and a number of approaches to the content are encouraged.

It is recognized that each classroom will represent a wide range in student activities. The social studies probably affords the teacher the greatest opportunity to meet these individual needs. Positive reference has been made to particular activities for accelerated, gifted, or keenly interested students. These activities are marked on the following guides with an asterisk (*).

The utilization of the problem-solving technique as exemplified by the scientific method needs to be embodied in each classroom situation. Although the nature of the approach will vary from kindergarten to the 12th grade, its important role in the learning process will prove invaluable to the student. The problem-solving technique coupled with the thrill of learning the *why* of his surroundings, as well as the *how* will contribute greatly to an individual's total development.

Due to the changing body of knowledge about man and his surroundings, the social studies curriculum in the Vancouver Public Schools must be thought of as being dynamic. For this reason activities and materials used in the classroom may vary from the ones listed. Teachers are encouraged to note better reference materials and proposed guide changes. These modifications can then be incorporated in future guides and the appropriate materials purchased.

Overview for the 9th-Grade Social Studies Curriculum

The 9th-grade program is divided into two distinct areas of subject matter. The area for one semester is Comparative World Cultures; the area for the other is Washington. The latter is divided into three units:

> Government
> History
> Resources and Vocational Opportunities

The semester on Washington State is part of a state requirement for graduation from high school. Because Washington history is already a part of the curriculum at the 3rd- and 4th-grade levels, the 9th-grade acts as a review and an enrichment of information previously gained. The material studied, obviously, is more detailed and comprehensive. Major emphasis should be placed on the new areas of government and economic geography. The government unit is a continuation at the state level of the 8th-grade study of civics at the national level. The resources area investigates the economic and vocational possibilities of the state. This unit should help the student in planning his senior high school program.

The other semester involves an introduction to world cultures. Preston James' seven cultural areas seem to be a workable division that is subject to revision. In any case, the emphasis is on the economic and cultural, not on the geography of countries. Because the 6th and 7th grade areas are those of the Eastern and the Western Hemispheres, the 9th-grade is more concerned with ways of living (i.e., cultures) than with the place geography of the countries.

The emphasis for these seven cultural areas is on a survey of economic progress, social organizations, languages, growth in nationalism, influence of religious philosophy, or on aesthetic contributions. Time is limited, and it would be manifestly impossible to cover all these facets. An economic approach is presently being emphasized.

Resource units on each of the areas have been compiled and are provided from the Curriculum Office. The units are distributed to new teachers during the orientation workshop.

Suggested Time Plan for the 9th Grade

One Semester

Washington Government	7 weeks
Washington History	5 weeks
Washington Resources	6 weeks

One Semester

Europe	2½ weeks
North Africa and Southwest Asia	3 weeks
Africa	3 weeks
Soviet	2 weeks
Orient	3 weeks
Pacific	1½ weeks
Americas	3 weeks

Sample Material—Grade 9

Grade Level Theme—Washington State Government and History
Resource Unit Title—Washington State History

Preface

This resource unit on Washington History is prepared to satisfy a state requirement for the study of the history of the state. Because the time allotted does not make possible an intensive investigation of all aspects of our early history, the approach is a simple one. It would be manifestly impossible to look into all the study activities mentioned in the unit, but it is hoped that every teacher will find ones suitable for his particular situation. The approach lends itself to a variety of techniques; this area seems particularly well suited to team teaching. The class may be divided into committees which prepare panel discussions.

The study of Washington History is followed by an intensive study of present day city, county, and state government.

General Objectives

- To review the part that each nation played in the exploration of the area
- To evaluate the contributions of the fur traders
- To appreciate the contributions of the missionaries to the settlement of the area
- To follow the transition from fur trading to farming
- To analyze the basic needs for the organization of government
- To review the contributions of individual men to the early history of the state
- To find out how law and order were developed in the territory
- To learn the process by which a territory becomes a state
- To learn the process by which an area becomes a territory
- To ascertain the reasons for our separation from the Oregon Territory
- To evaluate treaties made with the Indians
- To map the wagon and railroad surveys through the mountains
- To become familiar with stories of "The Heroic Age" in Washington history
- To improve basic language skills
- To become familiar with Washington literature

Specific Objectives

- To review early explorations
- To appreciate the contributions of the missionaries
- To evaluate the contributions of the fur companies
- To define terms of government
- To find out how law and order were established in the Northwest

Grade 9   Grade Level Theme: *Washington State Government & History*. Resource Unit Title: *Washington State History*. Major Objectives: *To review early explorations by sea.*

CONCEPTS	LEARNING ACTIVITIES (includes skills)	REFERENCES
Many nations were seeking the Northwest Passage.	Teacher should *explain* what was going on in Europe at this time.	*A History of the Pacific Northwest*, p. 46.
	Define Northwest Passage.	*History of the State of Washington*, p. 3.
	Chart the early explorations chronologically including name of country, date, name of explorer, area explored, and importance of exploration.	*History of the State of Washington*, Chapter one.
		Northwest Explorations, pp. 33–104.
		Empire of the Columbia, pp. 37–78.
	Divide the above by countries.	
		A History of the Pacific Northwest, pp. 42–56.
	List the reasons that people first came to the Northwest.	
	Name the explorations on which different countries based their claims to this area.	See above listings.
	Discuss French and Portuguese explorations.	*History of the State of Washington*, p. 12.
	Tell the Juan de Fuca story.	*History and Government of the State of Washington*, pp. 69–72.
	List the "firsts."	*History of the State of Washington*, pp. 4–5.
The Spanish made many important voyages. Balboa Cabrillo Ferello Perez Heceta Quadra	*Relate* the importance of each of the men who sailed under the flag of Spain.	*History of the State of Washington*, pp. 5–6.
	Create a painting of a conquistador.	*Northwest Explorations*, pp. 31–33, 71–91.
	Read Barto and Fuller on the Spanish explorers.	
The Russians were pioneers in the fur trade. Bering Chirikov Pribilof Baranof	*Read* Barto and one other authority on Russian explorations.	*Northwest Explorations*, pp. 55–77.
	Review reasons for the Russians' coming to the Northwest and importance of their explorations.	*Northwest Explorations*, p. 78.
	Explain the reasons that they were not among those who laid claim to the continental area.	
The English also appeared early on the Pacific Coast. Drake Cook Meares Vancouver	*Read* two authorities on the English explorations. *Tell* the name of Drake's flagship.	*History of the State of Washington* can be used as reference for most of these activities. It will not be listed hereafter.
	Construct a model of an early ship.	

Grade 9   Grade Level Theme: *Washington State Government & History*. Resource Unit Title: *Washington State History*. Major Objectives: *To review early explorations by sea.*

Create a painting of one.

Tell the story of the Nootka Sound Controversy. Locate Nootka Sound.	*A History of the Pacific Northwest*, pp. 47–48.
	The Great Northwest, p. 25.
Discuss the places that Vancouver visited.	*Northwest Explorations*, pp. 129–150.
	A History of the Pacific Northwest, pp. 44–45.
Make a *list* of areas that he named.	
Locate Deception Bay.	*Northwest Explorations*, pp. 121, 159.
Name the person who supervised the building of the Northwest America, first ship launched on the Northwest Coast.	*Northwest Explorations*, p. 115.
Indicate the problems involved in such a project.	
Indicate the importance of Cook's expeditions.	*History and Government of the State of Washington*, p. 77.
Tell what happened to Cook.	

After the establishment of the United States, the Americans became interested in trading in the Northwest. 　　Ledyard 　　Gray 　　Kendrick	Teacher should *remind* students of the fact that discovery and exploration were incidental to trade.	*Empire of the Columbia*, p. 36.
	Investigate the importance of Ledyard, our first publicity agent.	*The Great Northwest*, p. 27.
	Give the *names* of Gray's ships.	
	State the *purpose* of the Americans' trip to the coast.	*Empire of the Columbia*, pp. 65–66.
	Give the *date* of the discovery of the Columbia.	*Northwest Explorations*, pp. 151–152.
	**Analyze* the importance of this discovery.	*Empire of the Columbia*, p. 71.
	Draw a map locating early explorations.	
Our heritage from the past should always be emphasized.	**List* the qualities necessary to a pioneer.	
	Teacher should *impress* on students a pride in our heritage.	

Grade 9   Grade Level Theme: *Washington State Government & History.* Resource Unit Title: *Washington State History.* Major Objective: *To review early land explorations.*

CONCEPTS	LEARNING ACTIVITIES (includes skills)	REFERENCES

The pioneer explorers by land were led by the English and the Americans.
    Alexander Mackenzie
    David Thompson
    Lewis and Clark
    Simon Fraser
	Prepare a panel, including some of the following:
	
	Name the first white man to cross the North American continent north of Mexico.
		Northwest Explorations, p. 216.

	Define cartographer.	
	Evaluate Thompson's map making.	*Empire of the Columbia*, pp. 112–115.
	Explain the importance of recording accomplishments.	
	*Compare the personalities and characters of these men.	*Northwest Explorations.*
		A History of the Pacific Northwest.
	*Explain them so that they seem like people, not pages in a book.	
	*Prepare a bibliography of material used to support two preceding activities.	Individual biographies.
	Locate the areas covered by these people.	
	Give interesting facts about Lewis and Clark.	John Hancock Co. pamphlet— *Lewis and Clark.*
	Evaluate the individual explorations.	
		Pictorial History of the State of Washington, pp. 20–24.

Grade 9   Grade Level Theme: *Washington State Government & History*. Resource Unit Title: *Washington State History*. Major Objective: *To compare the Indians of the area.*

CONCEPTS	LEARNING ACTIVITIES (includes skills)	REFERENCES

There were two main groups of Indians in what is now the state of Washington.	*Prepare* a report comparing the coast and the plateau Indians as to
	     appearance
	     social organization
	     housing
	     food
	     clothing
	     mode of travel
	     language
	     social customs.
		Empire of the Columbia, pp. 7–19.
		
		History and Government of the State of Washington, pp. 26–58.
		
		Readings in Pacific History, pp. 25–40.
		
		A History of the Pacific Northwest, pp. 21–41.

The modern Indian is a word.	*Locate* the early Indian tribes.	*History and Government of the State of Washington*, pp. 224, 242.
	Explain the Chinook Jargon.	
	Investigate the provisions for their education.	*A History of the Pacific Northwest*, pp. 40–41. Write Department of Indian Affairs, Portland.
	Analyze some of the problems of adjustment to our society.	*American Indian.*
	Prepare a debate on the subject: Resolved that the American Indian was treated fairly.	

Grade 9   Grade Level Theme: *Washington State Government & History*. Resource Unit Title: *Washington State History*. Major Objective: *To evaluate the contributions of the fur companies.*

CONCEPTS	LEARNING ACTIVITIES (includes skills)	REFERENCES
Exploration in the Pacific Northwest was closely tied with the fur trade.	*Read* at least two authorities on the fur trade.	See bibliography.
	Report to the class on reading.	
	Make brief *annotations* on reading.	
The British fur companies maintained a more permanent organization in the Northwest.	*Prepare* a panel on the British fur companies. Include information on the following topics:	*The Great Northwest.*
		Empire of the Columbia.
	Give a brief history of the origin of the Hudson's Bay and the Northwest Fur Companies.	*A History of the Pacific Northwest.*
		Northwest Explorations.
	Characterize the type of people who maintained the fur business.	*Empire of the Columbia*, p. 80.
	Contrast the business methods of the two companies.	*Northwest Explorations*, pp. 322–328.
	Describe a brigade.	*A History of the Pacific Northwest*, pp. 90–91.
	Review establishment at Fort Vancouver.	*Empire of the Columbia.*
	Explain the fort system.	
	Locate some of the forts.	*Fort Vancouver.*
	Visit Fort Vancouver National Monument.	
	Name some of the greatest factors.	
	Listen to a local historian.	*A History of the Pacific Northwest*, pp. 110–113.
	Give a brief report on some of the outstanding men.	*Northwest Explorations*, pp. 329–341.
	Report on the agriculture and cattle raising.	*A History of the Pacific Northwest*, pp. 112–115.
		Empire of the Columbia, pp. 161–162.
The bitter business rivalry between the two British companies led to their forced union under the Hudson's Bay Company.	*Discuss* relations with missionaries.	
	Investigate methods of competition.	
	Look up the Seven Oaks Massacre.	*Northwest Explorations*, pp. 322–328.
	Review the terms of union.	*City of the Rivers*, pp. 14–85.
The Hudson's Bay Company ultimately withdrew from what is now the state of Washington.	*Discuss* reasons for the decline of the fur trade.	*History and Government of the State of Washington*, pp. 105–107.
	Indicate terms of withdrawal.	
	Catalogue present day interests of the Hudson's Bay Company.	

Grade 9 Grade Level Theme: *Washington State Government & History*. Resource Unit Title: *Washington State History*. Major Objective: *To evaluate the contributions of the fur companies.*

An era can be studied through literature.	Librarian or teacher or group of students display samples of literature of period. Each student should choose at least one book to read and report on. Particular emphasis should be laid on biography.	See attached bibliography.
The American fur trade was led by the Astorians.	*Have* reports on the sea party.	*Readings in Pacific History*, pp. 41–66.
	Identify Thorn and Tonquin.	*Northwest Explorations*, pp. 279–299.
		Stories of the Far West, pp. 46–55.
		A History of the Pacific Northwest, pp. 95–100.
	Tell the story of the land party.	
	Analyze the reasons for the failure of the land party.	*Northwest Explorations*, pp. 300–315.
		Stories of the Far West, pp. 55–70.
	List leaders of the expedition.	
	Read about the ordeal of Dorion's wife.	*Stories of the Far West*, pp. 69–70.
	Contrast her story with that of Sacajawea.	*A History of the Pacific Northwest*, p. 80.
	Discuss the conclusion of Astor's part of the fur trade.	
	Analyze the political importance of Astor's experiment.	*A History of the Pacific Northwest*, p. 109.
The Rocky Mountain Fur Company, a very loose business organization, was the most famous for its colorful personnel.	*List* the owners of the Rocky Mountain Fur Company from Ashley and Henry to Bridger.	*Northwest Explorations*, pp. 320–364.
	Describe the business organization.	*Northwest Explorations*, pp. 320–364.
	Write a story of a visit to a rendezvous.	*Empire of the Columbia*, pp. 165–166.
	List famous mountain men and their contributions.	
	Relate colorful stories about the mountain men.	*Trapper Days.*
	Draw a picture of a mountain man.	*Stories of the Far West.*
	Paint a mural of a rendezvous.	Individual biographies.
	Analyze reasons that so many of the mountain men came from the South.	
	List reasons for the decline of the Rocky Mountain Fur Company.	*Northwest Explorations*, pp. 357–358.
	Discuss its contributions to the Northwest.	*Northwest Explorations*, pp. 362–364.
	Visit meeting of Vancouver Historical Society.	

Grade 9 Grade Level Theme: *Washington State Government & History*. Resource Unit Title: *Washington State History*. Major Objective: *To appreciate the contributions of the missionaries.*

CONCEPTS	LEARNING ACTIVITIES (includes skills)	REFERENCES
The next steps toward statehood were taken by the missionaries.	*Locate* Lee's mission.	
	Give present name of the school that he established.	*The Great Northwest*, pp. 207–208.
The Rev. Jason Lee was the first to establish a mission in the Northwest.	*Discuss* original policy of school.	*Pictorial History of the State of Washington*, p. 42.
	Give reasons for success of Lee's mission.	*Pictorial History of the State of Washington*, p. 41.
	Locate first religious services held west of the Rockies.	*Pictorial History of the State of Washington*.
		Empire of the Columbia, pp. 208–211.
	Evaluate Lee's part in the establishment of government.	*Pictorial History of the State of Washington*, pp. 41–43.
The Whitmans made the first missionary settlement in what is now the state of Washington.	*Locate* the Whitman Mission.	
	Tell the meaning of the word, Waiilatpu.	*Empire of the Columbia*, p. 124.
	Evaluate the Whitman mission plan.	*Pioneer Education in the Pacific Northwest*, pp. 57–64.
		Empire of the Columbia, pp. 124–126.
		Pioneer Teachers of Washington, pp. 31–33.
	Discuss the use of irrigation by Dr. Whitman.	*Empire of the Columbia*, pp. 250, 252, 374.
	Tell about the importance of Dr. Whitman's plan to bring a wagon over the mountains.	*The Great Northwest*, p. 118.
		The Evergreen Land, p. 29.
	Tell about the Whitmans' help to the immigrants.	*Empire of the Columbia*, pp. 131–132.
		Oregon Trail.
	List the reasons for dissatisfaction among the Cayuse Indians with whom the Whitmans worked.	*Empire of the Columbia*, pp. 125, 130, 134, 136. *Pictorial History of the State of Washington*, p. 45.
	*Justify the statement "The fact that Dr. Whitman was a doctor was a disadvantage in his missionary efforts." 1. Indians' attitude toward their own medicine men. 2. Indians' failure to take medicine as directed.	
	Tell about Whitman Massacre.	*A History of the Pacific Northwest*, pp. 146–154.

Grade 9   Grade Level Theme: *Washington State Government & History*. Resource Unit Title: *Washington State History*. Major Objective: *To appreciate the contributions of the missionaries.*

	Evaluate the contributions of the Whitman missionary effort.	*Empire of Columbia*, p. 138.
	Contrast the methods of approach of the Indians used by Father DeSmet and Rev. Lee.	*Pioneer Education in the Pacific Northwest*, pp. 64–85.
		The Great Northwest, p. 119.
	List the contributions that Father DeSmet made toward the establishment of law and order.	
	Explain the way that the American government honored him.	*History and Government of the State of Washington*, p. 141.
	Explain the statement, "The Indians did not fear the Catholic Fathers because the latter did not encourage white settlement."	*History and Government of the State of Washington*, p. 139.
Father Blanchet was the originator of visual education in the Northwest.	*Discuss* the use of the Catholic Ladder and Sahale Stick.	*Pioneer Education in the Pacific Northwest*, p. 64.
	Try to find a picture of one.	*A History of the Pacific Northwest*, p. 136.
		History and Government of the State of Washington, p. 139.
After his arrival in the Oregon country, Father Blanchet did a great deal of work with the French Canadians.	*Discuss* Father Blanchet and the establishment of government.	*Empire of the Columbia*, p. 221.
		Readings in Pacific History, pp. 76–84.
	Tell about his educational work. (Blanchet House in Portland was named for him.)	*A History of the Pacific Northwest*, p. 196.

Grade 9   Grade Level Theme: *Washington State Government & History*. Resource Unit Title: *Washington State History*. Major Objective: *To find out how law and order were established in the Northwest.*

CONCEPTS	LEARNING ACTIVITIES (includes skills)	REFERENCES
The underlying cause for the establishment of a government in the Northwest was the need for united authority.	*Discuss* the reasons why the Hudson's Bay Company did not offer adequate protection to the Americans.	*Oregon Country* (sound film).
	Explain the provisions of the treaty of Joint Occupancy.	*History and Government of the State of Washington*, p. 145.
	Give reasons why such an arrangement would be unsatisfactory.	*The Great Northwest*, p. 150.
	Develop list of reasons why rules of conduct are necessary in any society of people.	
	Discuss specific areas in which formal government was necessary.	*History and Government of the State of Washington*, p. 146.
The immediate cause for the establishment of government in the Northwest was the death of Ewing Young.	*Read* the story about this wealthy man's death and the necessity for care for his 600 cattle.	*A History of the Pacific Northwest*, p. 196.
A series of meetings were held to discuss government.	*Discuss* the wolf meetings. *Tell* what happened at Champoeg.	*History and Government of the State of Washington*, p. 150.
	Identify the first American political figure.	*Stories of the Far West*, p. 168.
	Discuss Wilkes' attitude toward a government.	*History and Government of the State of Washington*, p. 148.
	Explain why Father Blanchet would not be interested in American government.	

Grade 9　Grade Level Theme: *Washington State Government & History*. Resource Unit Title: *Washington State History*. Major Objective: *To find out how law and order were established in the Northwest.*

	Justify the stand of the French Canadians who had settled south of the Willamette.	*Empire of the Columbia.*
	Describe Joe Meek's part in the proceedings.	*Stories of the Far West*, pp. 189–190.
A provisional government was established.	*Define* provisional.	*History and Government of the State of Washington*, p. 151.
	Explain provisions of early constitution.	
	Indicate changes made after trial.	
	List important officers of the provisional government and their duties.	
Agitation for a more permanent status soon occurred.	*Ascertain* some of the reasons for dissatisfaction with the provisional government.	*History and Government of the State of Washington*, pp. 153–154.
	Investigate the steps by which a territory is established.	
	Define territory.	
	Define Organic Act.	
	Explain Donation Land Act.	*Empire of the Columbia*, pp. 290–292.
	Discuss McLoughlin's change of attitude.	*History and Government of the State of Washington*, p. 154.
	Discuss the problem about the boundary and its solution.	*Empire of the Columbia.*
Oregon territory was created August 13, 1848.	*Identify* the first governor of Oregon Territory.	*A History of the Pacific Northwest*, pp. 176–178.
	List some of the problems and tell how he solved them.	*Empire of the Columbia*, pp. 294–295.

Grade 9   Grade Level Theme: *Washington State Government & History*. Resource Unit Title: *Washington State History*. Major Objective: *To learn of the creation of Washington Territory.*

CONCEPTS	LEARNING ACTIVITIES (includes skills)	REFERENCES
The settlers north of the Columbia were dissatisfied with the government of Oregon Territory.	*List* the reasons for dissatisfaction among the settlers north of the Columbia. *Justify* their dissatisfaction.	*History and Government of the State of Washington*, pp. 162–163. *Readings in Pacific History*, pp. 119–129.
Agitation for the division of Oregon Territory inevitably followed.	*Write* a brief summary of the Cowlitz Convention.	*History and Government of the State of Washington*, pp. 163–164.
	Summarize the Monticello Convention in the same manner.	
	Ascertain the attitude of the officials of Oregon Territory.	*Readings in Pacific History*, pp. 113–115.
	Discuss the memorial seeking division of territory.	
	Discuss territorial government.	*Readings in Pacific History*, pp. 131–154.
	State the date of creation and the boundaries of Washington Territory.	*History and Government of the State of Washington*, p. 164.

Grade 9   Grade Level Theme: *Washington State Government & History*. Resource Unit Title: *Washington State History*. Major Objective: *To become familiar with the establishment of Washington State.*

CONCEPTS	LEARNING ACTIVITIES (includes skills)	REFERENCES
Territorial governor Stevens had two major problems. One of them was a railroad survey.	*Discuss* the problems connected with the railroad survey.	*A History of the Pacific Northwest,* pp. 206–210.
	Trace mountain passes on an outline map.	
	Develop story of the break between Stevens and McClellan.	
	Read about the conclusion of the surveys.	
The second problem was one of making treaties with the Indians.	*Read* at least two authoritative stories of the first Walla Walla Council.	*Readings in Pacific History,* pp. 85–105.
	Decide what was accomplished.	*A History of the Pacific Northwest,* pp. 220–223. *History and Government of the State of Washington,* pp. 167–169.
	Divide the Indian tribes into the friendly and the unfriendly ones.	*The Great Northwest,* p. 174.
	Characterize different leaders.	
	Obtain pictures of famous Indian chiefs who attended the council.	
	Summarize accomplishments of other councils.	*A History of the Pacific Northwest,* pp. 239–240.
The councils did not solve the Indian problem.	*Discuss* causes of Indian uprisings.	*Readings in Pacific Northwest History,* pp. 85–102.
	State reasons why the Indians justified their ignoring the treaties.	*The Evergreen Land,* pp. 37–39. *A History of the Pacific Northwest,* p. 221.
	Appoint a committee to report to the class on the Indian Wars west of the Cascades.	*The Great Northwest,* pp. 171–177, pp. 250–252. *History and Government of the State of Washington,* pp. 166–174.
	Appoint a committee to report to the class on the war east of the Cascades.	*Pacific Northwest Indian Wars.*
	List the leaders.	*The Evergreen Land,* pp. 36–39.
	Read Chief Joseph's speech aloud.	Excerpt—*History and Government of the State of Washington,* p. 183.
	Discuss the treaties.	*Hear Me My Chiefs.* *A History of the Pacific Northwest,* pp. 213–272.
	*Justify provisions for the Indians.	*Empire of the Columbia,* pp. 306–308.

Grade 9   Grade Level Theme: *Washington State Government & History.* Resource Unit Title: *Washington State History.* Major Objective: *To become familiar with the establishment of Washington State.*

The territory advanced toward statehood.	*Discuss* problems due to size and topography.	*Readings in Pacific History*, pp. 131–151.

	Investigate political and •social conditions
	        Chinese riots
	        women suffrage, etc.
		History and Government of the State of Washington, pp. 197–199.

Education has always been a matter of prime concern to Washingtonians.	*Locate* first school.	*History and Government of the State of Washington*, pp. 223–229.
	Give provisions and date of first school law.	
	**Read* about and report on pioneer teachers.	
	Ascertain name of first territorial superintendent of school.	
	Indicate growth in number of schools.	*Pioneer Education in the Pacific Northwest.*
	Report on institutions of higher learning.	*Pioneer Teachers of Washington.*
Washington was made a state on November 11, 1889.	*Discuss* the Enabling Act.	*History and Government of the State of Washington*, pp. 313–317.
	Review state constitution.	
	Compare with national constitution.	
	Read the State's Bill of Rights.	
	Give the name of the first governor.	
	Make a *list* of governors.	
	Learn the state song.	
Culmination.	*Draw* the state seal. Students give brief oral reports of library reading.	

Student Bibliography

The school libraries and the public library have excellent collections of material on this area. A partial list of them follows. The starred items are the more advanced reading. (See preceding unit guides for additions to student bibliography.)

Anderson, Eva	*A Child's History of Washington*	University Press	1953
Avery	*History and Government of the State of Washington*	University of Washington Press	1961
Babcock and Babcock	*Our Pacific Northwest*	McGraw Hill	1963
Barto and Bullard	*History of the State of Washington*	Heath	1957
Bibb	*History of Early Common School Education*	University Press	1929
Downie, Ralph	*A Pictorial History of the State of Washington*	Lowman	1937
Fargo, Lucille	*The Spokane Story*	Columbia	1950
*Fuller, George	*A History of the Pacific Northwest*	Binfords and Mort	1931
Gates, Charles M.	*Readings in Northwest History*	University Press	1941
*Johannsen and Gates	*Empire of the Columbia*	Harper	1957
Judson, Katherine	*Stories of the Old West*	Metropolis	1936
Masters, Joseph	*Stories of the Old West* (good for local color)	Ginn	1935
Speck, Gordon	*Northwest Explorations* (good for local color)	Binfords and Mort	1954
*Winther, Oscar	*The Great Northwest*	Knopf	1952

Map

Historic Pacific Northwest

Supplementary Bibliography

Anderson, Eva	*Chief Seattle*	Caxton	1943
Bakeless, John	*Adventures of Lewis and Clark* (easy)	Houghton Mifflin	1962
Balch, F. H.	*Bridge of the Gods*	Binfords and Mort	1940
*Barker, Burt B.	*Letters of Dr. John McLoughlin*	Metropolitan	1948
Brown, Jennie	*Fort Hall on the Oregon Trail*	Caxton	1932
Burt, Olive	*Jebediah Smith*	Messner	1951
Carr, Mary Jane	*Young Mac of Fort Vancouver* (easy reading)	Heath	1957
Case, Robert	*Empire Builders*	Binfords and Mort	1959
Daugherty, James	*Trappers and Traders of the Far West* (easy)	Hale	1952
Davis, Julia	*No Other White Man*	Dutton	1937

DeVoto, Bernard	*Journals of Lewis and Clark*	Houghton Mifflin	1953
Dye, Eva	*McLoughlin and Old Oregon*	McClurg	1936
Eaton, Jeanette	*Narcissa Whitman*	Harcourt, Brace	1941
Emmons, Della	*Nothing in Life Is Free*	Northwestern Press	1953
Emmons, Della	*Sacajawea of the Shoshones* (easy)	Binfords and Mort	1948
Farnsworth, Cecil	*Winged Moccasins*	Messner	1954
Frazee, Steve	*Year of the Big Snow*	Holt (Fremont)	1962
Garst, Shannon	*Joe Meek*	Messner	1948
*Howard, John	*War Chief Joseph*	Caxton	1946
Johnson, Robert	*John McLoughlin*	Metropolitan	1935
Lampman, Evelyn	*Princess of Fort Vancouver*	Doubleday	1962
Mason, Miriam	*Young Mr. Meeker*	Bobbs, Merril	1952
Montgomery, Richard	*White Head Eagle*	Macmillan	1934
Morgan, Dale	*Jed Smith*	Bobbs, Merril	1953
Neuberger, Richard	*The Lewis and Clark Expedition* (easy)	Random House	1951
Parkman, Francis	*The Oregon Trail*	Grosset	1927
Roberts, Mary	*Wagon Trail of '43*	Exposition	1961
Schultz, J. W.	*Bird Woman* (easy)	Houghton Mifflin	1918
Sheller, Roscoe	*Ben Snipes, Northwest Cattle King*	Binfords Mort	1957
Spencer, Omar	*The Story of Sauvies Island*	Metropolitan	1950
Skinner, Constance	*Beaver, Kings and Cabins*	Macmillan	1940
*Spawln, A. J.	*Kamiakin*	Binfords Mort	1944
Stelle, William	*Westward Adventure*	Harcourt	1962
Strong, Thomas	*Cathlamet on the Columbia*	Metropolitan Press	1952
Thompson, Margaret	*On the Trail with Lewis and Clark*	Exposition Press	1952
Van Den Loeff, Rutgers	*Oregon at Last*	Morrow	1961

Bibliography Unit II

Additional Supplementary

Allred and others	*Great Western Indian Fights*	Doubleday	1960
Blackwelder, Bernice	*Great Westerner*	Caxton	1960
Bowden, Angie	*Early Schools in Washington Territory*	Lowman and Hanford	1935
Daniels, Walter	*American Indians*	Wilson	1957
Daugherty, James	*Of Courage Undaunted*	Viking	1951
Downey, Fairfax	*Indian Wars*	Doubleday	1963
Fraser, Hermia	*Toll Brigade*	Binfords and Mort	nd
Fuller, Iola	*The Loon Feather*	Harcourt	nd
Glasey, R. H.	*Pacific Northwest Indian Wars*	Binfords and Mort	1953
Hagan, W. H.	*American Indians*	University of Chicago	1961

Hazard, Joseph T.	*Pioneer Teachers of Washington*	Lowman and Hanford	1955
Holbrook and others	*The Pacific Northwest*	Doubleday	1963
Hussey, John	*History of Fort Vancouver*	Washington Historical Society	1957
La Farge, Oliver	*American Indian*	Golden Press	nd
Lucia, Ellis	*Saga of Ben Halliday*	Historical Society of Montana	1962
MacDonald, Lucile	*Search for the Northwest Passage*	Binfords and Mort	1958
Margaret, Helene	*Father DeSmet*	Farrar and Rinehart	1940
Marriot, Alice	*The First Comers*	Longmans	1960
McWhorter, L. V.	*Hear Me My Chiefs*	Caxton	1962
National Park Service	*Soldier and Brave*	Harper and Row	1963
Peery, W. K.	*And There Were Salmon*	Binfords and Mort	1949
	(This book is out of print but is probably in most of the libraries. It is for the reluctant reader and is popular with him.)		
Peery, W. K.	*Silver Streams*	Metropolitan	1936
Ross, Nancy Wilson	*Westward the Women*	Random House	1958
Wellman, Paul	*The Indian Wars of the West*	Doubleday	1963
Wissler, Clark	*American Indian*	Smith	nd

Periodical

| Montana | *The Magazine of Western History* | Helena, Montana |

Sound Films

CWSC	*The Oregon Trail*	Encyclopedia Britannica Film
WSU	*U. S. Expansion*	*Settling the West*
WSU	*U. S. Expansion*	*Oregon Country*

Evaluation

Any social studies unit should be in constant revision—there are changes in our world even as the words describing one state of affairs are being written. Evaluation is also a continuous process. There should be almost daily teacher-pupil evaluation, as has already been mentioned in the learning activities. The pupils and the teacher should appraise their achievements of the day and decide what they need to do the next day.

Various evaluating procedures may be used including written tests of both the objective and essay type; evaluation or oral and written work by the pupil himself, by other pupils, and by the teacher. The teacher should ask himself:

Am I helping students to grow in their ability to evaluate their own work?

Is each student working up to his own potential?

Am I using standardized social studies tests to evaluate growth?

Am I integrating the various other subjects when I can sensibly do so?

Have I tried to include all the concepts (geographic, historic, economic, cultural, etc.)?

How adequately am I using the wide variety of source materials?

How much progress are the pupils making in the ability to participate in discussions?

Have pupils learned the basic research skills?

Am I providing opportunity for creative writing?

Are pupils learning to read more analytically?

Have pupils satisfactorily increased their social studies vocabulary?

Have students acquired an adequate knowledge of the specific objectives of the unit?

Chapter 5

8th Grade Social Studies

Robinson Junior High School, Wichita, Kansas*

The Wichita Public School System, in its effort to promote and perpetuate the American way of life, accepts the following ideals as basic to its educational platform.[1]

The school system shall stress and inculcate the democratic way of life in order to perpetuate the ideals and principles embodied in the Declaration of Independence and in the Constitution.

The American public school system was founded to maintain and promote the American way of life. Education must serve liberty, justice, and equality of opportunity.

Education in the public schools of Wichita, in addition to assisting in the perpetuation of our democratic society, must serve the individual in the light of his capacities and abilities by providing a suitable and well-balanced learning environment in the areas of physical, mental, emotional, cultural, social, moral, and spiritual maturity.

The public schools in Wichita shall not only be concerned with knowledge of subject matter, but also concerned with an understanding of and an interest in children themselves—their growth, interests, needs, and unique personalities.

The Board of Education in Wichita should see that there is freedom to learn, with free access to information and free discussion with open avenues of communication.

The Wichita Public School System places great emphasis on the supreme worth and dignity of the individual consistent with the general welfare and common good.

Purposes of the Public Schools

The principal educational goals of the Wichita Public School System shall be:

Intellectual development
Self development
Citizenship development
Cultural development
Vocational development

Responsibilities of the Public Schools

The Wichita Public School System has some responsibility for educational leadership in the community. It is important that the school assist the home and other educational agencies through cooperative and supplementary measures. The responsibilities of the public schools are threefold. The public schools have (a) primary responsibility for some phases of education, (b) partial or shared responsibility for other phases of education, and (c) some responsibility for educational leadership in the community.

The primary responsibility of the public school is to teach the basic skills in learning and the mastery of content in the organized subject matter areas.

The shared responsibilities of the public schools include the following:

To inculcate an appreciation of and a loyalty to American institutions.

To develop proper habits and attitudes of study and work.

To accept responsibility for individual and group action.

To develop an understanding of the rights and duties of American citizenship.

To teach how to make better use of leisure time through the pursuit of individual interests and hobbies.

To develop appreciation for creativity in fine arts.

---

* Information supplied by Mr. Frederick H. Hale, Social Studies Teacher, Robinson Junior High School, Wichita, Kansas.

[1] *Personnel Policies for the Classroom Teacher,* Wichita Public School System, 1963, pp. 1–2.

To develop and promote economic and social competency.

To provide an adequate program of individual and group guidance.

To develop sound bodies with good physical and mental health habits.

To develop an appreciation of worthy home membership.

Point of View of the Social Studies

The philosophy of the social studies curriculum is drawn from and supports the general aims and objectives of the Wichita Public Schools. A major goal is the development of citizens who function effectively in a democratic society by giving each individual the education which his talents and capabilities warrant.

More specifically, the social studies are concerned with human problems arising out of man's contact with his physical environment and personal relationships with other people. For the purpose of this guide, this description of the social studies is illustrative.

The social studies are concerned with people and their interaction with their social and physical environment; they deal with human relationships. In the social studies, attention is given to ways of living and working together, use of environment to meet basic needs, customs, institutions, values and life situations—the cultural heritage and its dynamic on-going characteristics.[2]

The content of these studies is drawn from history, geography, political science, economics, sociology, psychology, anthropology, and related disciplines. The social studies attempt to provide students with reliable and useful knowledge, fundamental skills and desirable attitudes as a basis for satisfactory day-by-day experiences, and future effectiveness in their personal and civic life.

Common Objectives for the Social Studies, K–12

Understandings

The interdependence of people
Concepts of time, place, distance, and sequence of events
People of the community who contribute to better living
World happenings and problems
Ways to achieve and maintain personal health and safety

The conservation of natural resources
Geographic factors which influence ways of living in the world
Contributions of past cultures to our existing civilization
How change has occurred through developments in science, technology, and the arts
How democracy has developed in America and how it operates
The nature and importance of sound moral, spiritual, and aesthetic values
The American economic system and economic cooperation
The function of the individual in our democratic society

Attitudes

Respect for the feelings and rights of others
Respect for the property of others
Self-respect, self-discipline, and moral health
Satisfaction from personal achievement and group acceptance
Sense of loyalty to home, school, community, and nation
Acceptance of the need for orderly, responsible living in democratic society
Respect for the processes of democratic decision-making and differences of opinion of others
Appreciation and respect for people of different cultural, economic, and religious backgrounds
Appreciation for the work and labor of others
Appreciation of art, literature, music, and wholesome recreational activities

Skills

Expressing ideas and feelings
Listening, observing, speaking, and writing
Maintaining health, safety, personal and school property
Relating cause and effect
Study independently
Developing vocabulary
Participating in individual and group planning
Leading and following in a group
Locating and gathering information from many sources
Using library facilities
Organizing and analyzing information
Presenting data in written or oral form

Description of Grade Level Content

Kindergarten

Learning how to live at home and at school; school personnel; safety and health; transportation and conservation; members of the family and their work and play; special days of the year.

Grade 1

Learning about family and school life; how to keep safe and healthy; the homes of people; family work

[2] Michaelis, John U., *Social Studies for Children in a Democracy*. Second Edition. Englewood Cliffs, New Jersey: Prentice-Hall, Inc. 1956, p. 2.

and fun; helpers in the community; seasons and holidays.

Grade 2

How people travel and get their food and clothing; health and safety at work and play; people and resources of the community; time and special ways; uses of maps and globes.

Grade 3

Understanding community differences and the growth of communities; types of homes; concepts of time, distance, and the past; Indians and pioneers; history and community life in Wichita.

Grade 4

The geography and physical facts of different parts of the world; hot, cold, dry, mountainous lands; the way people live and adapt to their environment in these places.

Grade 5

The discovery of the American continents; their resources and climates; the settlement and growth of the United States; geography, history, economic, and social facts of all regions.

Grade 6

Canada, Latin America, and Europe; geographic facts about the parts of each area; history of settlement; use of resources; growth of society to present status.

Grade 7—Social Living

Cultures and contributions of major nations of the world; major emphasis on their geographic features with sketches of their history; correlated with language arts content.

Grade 8—American History

Exploration and development to the present; political, military, and social history; growth and problems of industrial and international power to 1870.

Grade 9—Civics

Civic knowledge of local and national political organization; the economic system and state history; personal-social understanding of occupations, the home, and other social institutions.

Grade 9—World History

Earliest civilization to the present; development and achievements of western civilization; the emergence of democracy; international problems of the twentieth century.

Grade 10—World History

Elective course with the same general organization and content as in grade 9.

Grade 11—United States History

The establishment and growth of the nation; its principles, cultural values, and varied resources; interpretations of political, social, economic, and international conflicts in the American experience, from 1870 to the present.

Grade 12—United States Government

Institutions and practices of American government and society; basic philosophy and values; patterns of political organization; the political process and civil rights; domestic and international realities.

The Guide

The Guide is the culmination of a curriculum study which involved many committees, individuals, and consultants. The membership on the various committees represented all grade levels. In different ways elementary and secondary social studies teachers, supervisors, and administrators made a contribution to the curriculum study.

The social studies guide encompasses all grade levels from kindergarten through grade 12, including all state required offerings and the additional secondary world history elective which is offered in grades 9 and 10. As such, it is designed as a descriptive, vertical framework, giving continuity to instruction and containing the social studies components of general education for the Wichita Public Schools.

The guide represents an attempt to define the sequential course of development and the teaching of necessary and useful social knowledge by allocating specialized responsibilities and subject content to the respective grades or levels. The unit pattern is used as the basis for content organization throughout, with each grade or course having a succession of units. The number of units comprising each course or grade has been kept relatively small in the conviction that the desired depth and intensity of learning will more likely result from such a design.

It is intended that the use of this guide will provide social studies teachers with a broader perspective of the total program, a clearer view of their own important position in the program, and a rich variety of materials and teaching procedures to use in their own planning.

Implicit in the guiding philosophy which spawns such curriculum materials is the recognition that they serve an equally useful purpose by providing the foundation from which continuous curriculum improvement may proceed.

Pattern of Unit Organization

I. The pattern of unit organization is as follows:
   A. Title
   B. Statement of significance
   C. Specific unit objectives
      1. Understandings
      2. Attitudes
      3. Skills
   D. Scope of the unit—this is presented in the form of a content outline suggesting major points of emphasis in topical or question style
   E. Unit activities
      1. Introductory
      2. Developmental
      3. Culminating
      4. Evaluative—suggestions for evaluation are included in some units and omitted in others; the general statement on evaluation is applicable to units in all grades
   F. Resource materials
      1. Reading materials
      2. Audio-visual aids
      3. Community resources
      4. Music (Songs)
II. Usually more activities are suggested than could or should be used by any teacher during the course of a single unit. The selection of certain ones for use is left to the individual teacher.
III. The resource materials listed with each unit of a grade may accomplish a dual purpose. Serving first as a reservoir of useful materials from which to draw in developing teaching plans for specific units, they also offer an opportunity for the entire grade from the recurrent listings of certain textbooks and other references in the different units.

Grade 8—General Objectives

I. General Understandings of:
   A. Our American heritage and how, because of our background, we have cultural differences
   B. The story of our nation and its development into a world power
   C. Our government and the duties and responsibilities of American citizenship
   D. The price paid for freedom and how we have come to believe in American democracy and develop loyalty to it
   E. World problems and why American citizens need to be informed about world affairs
II. General Attitudes of:
   A. Realizing the importance of cooperation and self-restraint in our personal, national, and international endeavor
   B. Respect for the rights and beliefs of other people
   C. Tolerance for minority groups and differences in cultural backgrounds of all peoples
   D. Respect for law and justice and the desire to maintain the American way of life
   E. World-mindedness and a willingness to do one's share in school, community, and other social environments
III. General Skills in:
   A. Developing fundamental processes of reading, writing, spelling, and vocabulary improvement
   B. The ability to listen, take notes, and follow directions
   C. Map reading, uses of charts and globes, and interpreting geographical information
   D. Self-expression in group discussion, oral reporting, and writing activities
   E. The use of research methods and library facilities

Suggestions for Using Resource Units

The resource units comprising the curriculum guide are consistent with the viewpoint stated earlier, and have been developed with the expressed purpose of offering assistance to teachers in their efforts to achieve the objectives of the social studies program.

A resource unit has been described as a "teaching file" containing materials, ideas, and suggestions from which a teacher may prepare a unit for classroom purposes. Resource units are not designed to be taught as developed, but rather to serve as "resources." It is assumed that the teaching unit can be planned only by an individual teacher with reference to his own experience and personality and to his students and their abilities.

The units and courses presented herein are, therefore, considered as guides and "starting places" for the teacher.

In our Wichita Public Schools our 8th-grade American History and 11th-grade American History classes complement each other in that we have split them in regard to the time aspect: At the 8th-grade level we study American History from colonization through 1870 in some depth—in the past it had been largely an overview from colonization to modern times; in the junior year the course reviews briefly the colonization period, then covers in depth from 1870 to modern times. We have been using this concept since 1962–63 and it seems to be working well. The idea behind this concept is to eliminate any needless overlapping of subject matter material.[3]

A Resource Unit for 8th-Grade American History

Unit I—The Geographic and Historic Setting

I. *Significance of the Topic Area*: The purpose of this introductory unit is to provide the student with a reason for the study of history, an overview of the course, and a firm foundation in geographical concepts valuable for the study of American history.

---

[3] Comments supplied by Mr. Frederick H. Hale, Social Studies Instructor, Robinson Junior High School, Wichita, Kansas.

Emphasis is given to the study of the three-eighths of the North American continent that makes up the mainland of the United States. Time is given to a review of the geography of the world and particularly the geographic features of Eurasia that led to the age of discovery and exploration.

Emphasis is given early in the unit to the use of the tools for learning geography and history such as maps, time lines, atlases, textbooks, charts, and graphs. The student must learn something of the land he lives on and a great deal of how people have been influenced by living on the land. Our main concern in this unit is geography.

II. *Inventory of Possible Objectives*: The objectives listed below have been divided into five general areas. (A) basic understandings, (B) skills, (C) attitudes, (D) interests, (E) appreciations. The purpose of this list is to provide an inventory from which a selection can be made based upon the needs of the group.

A. *Basic Understandings*: The pupil understands that:

1. History is a written record of change and development in man and his way of life.
2. Man's ideas, desires, and needs change and are changed by conditions of heredity, environment, and personal experiences.
3. The study of history requires the mastery of its tools such as maps, charts, graphs, indices, and time lines.
4. The geography of a country is a description of the surface of the land, its natural resources, climate, bodies of water, plant and animal life.
5. Natural harbors along the Atlantic coast provided shelter, protection, and convenience for early settlers. Many settlements at such places became our leading cities of today.
6. The colonists did not settle west of the Appalachians for 100 years, during which the mountains protected them and forced them into groups where a strong spirit of unity and strength developed.
7. Geography affects the way people make a living.
8. Soil and climate have affected our agricultural development.
9. Mineral resources have affected the growth of cities and the westward migration of population.
10. Geography has affected both the routes and the means of transportation in our country.
11. Geography has affected the distribution of the population.
12. Cities grew up along the fall line because of power and portage.
13. The United States can be divided into seven natural regions; the Atlantic Coastal Plain, the Piedmont, the Appalachian chain, Central Plains, Great Plains, Western Highlands, and the Pacific Coastal Region.

14. Geographical conditions were both a help and a hindrance to the westward movement.
15. Geography will prove to be a factor in the rise of regional differences in the new nation.
16. Man sometimes changes the face of the land or the course of rivers to meet his needs.
17. Geographic features of America are partly responsible for the strong spirit of independence and self-reliance that grew in early America.
18. Geography for our part of the world has had an effect on the character of the people.

B. *Skills*: Skills are recognized and accepted as important educational outcomes and are involved in this resource unit to the extent that the student should be able to:
1. Recognize the distinctive vocabulary of the social sciences.
2. Recognize the various map projections.
3. Use the time line as a tool for understanding history and master the concept of A.D. and B.C.
4. Use the textbook with reference to footnotes, the use of the index, the appendices, and the selected bibliography.
5. Use charts and graphs in interpreting history.
6. Recognize the major divisions of the earth in terms of hemispheres, latitudes, and longitudes.
7. Recognize the major bodies of water and major river systems of the world.
8. Recognize the geographic features of the world that separate the Old World from the New.
9. Recognize the lakes, bays, gulfs, river systems, and mountain ranges of North America.
10. Name and locate the states of the United States on an outline map.
11. Name and locate the seven natural regions of the United States.
12. Name and locate the climatic regions of the United States.
13. Name and locate the major cities of the United States such as: New York, Washington, D.C., Chicago, Kansas City, Minneapolis, St. Louis, New Orleans, Houston, Denver, Seattle, Los Angeles, and San Francisco.
14. Recognize areas of land fertility and suitability for farming in the United States.
15. Locate the deposits of natural resources in the United States.
16. Name the major river systems of the United States.

C. *Attitudes*: The use of the term *attitudes* in this resource unit shall be limited to *beliefs* or *opinions*, and not be specifically concerned with the attitudes of *cooperation, honesty,* or *toler-*

ance. Since objectives are used as a basis for evaluation, the teaching of attitudes in the sense of beliefs implies the testing of those beliefs. There is some question as to the precise role of the public school in the teaching of beliefs or the influence of individual opinions. Should the public school direct its attention to the beliefs or opinions of individuals in a democratic society? The experience level of junior high school students causes some difficulties for them to form opinions or beliefs of their own. A certain amount of indoctrination is unavoidable. The purpose of this set of objectives is to provide the student with a frame of reference from which he can learn to draw his own conclusions. These objectives are not limited to the first unit of the course and are set down here as a basis upon which to build. The student should show progress toward a belief in:
1. The inherent worth and dignity of every human being.
2. The ability of free men to rule themselves.
3. An equal opportunity for all in the pursuit of the good life.
4. Freedom within the framework of law.
5. The free enterprise system.
6. The importance of agreeing for the common good.

D. *Interests*: Possible areas of interest within the scope of this unit are unlimited except for the small amount of time devoted to the unit. A few suggestions are given below.
1. Construction of charts and graphs showing the growth of population in America from 1610 to 1960.
2. Construction of maps similar to those used by early explorers.
3. Committee work on geographic sections of the United States.
4. Map American folk lore and legends.
5. Prehistoric map of North America.
6. Begin a project of record keeping of the climate.
7. Book reports on related topics.
8. Construction of time-lines.

E. *Appreciations*: The story of America has many faces. The student should be encouraged to appreciate:
1. The efforts of early map makers to chart the world.
2. The great diversity of natural regions in America.
3. The growth of America.
4. The clinging to "bed-rock" beliefs in the American way.

III. Content Outline
A. *Expository Outline*: This is intended to suggest approximate amounts of time to be devoted to major objectives. The completion of the Unit will take the first two weeks of the school year. It will set the pace for the work to be done in the future.

1. Introduction of the textbook, orientation to class routine, and working on the first assignment will require a full class period.
2. Chapter I has two major divisions. The remainder of the week will be required to cover this material.
   a) Growth of a Nation, p. 12, a very short section. Could be read in class.
   b) Then and Now, pp. 12–26, lengthy for a single assignment. May require a day for reading and one for discussion.
   c) Review and evaluation will be in order for the remainder of the week.
3. Chapter II has three major divisions. It will require a time allotment of one week.
   a) The Importance of Geography to History, p. 28. This could be read aloud and discussed.
   b) How Geography Affected our Settlement, pp. 29–35. Attention is given here to the seven natural regions of the United States. Two days will be needed to cover this material, perhaps more.
   c) How Geography Affected our Development, pp. 36–42. The relationships between Geography and soil, climate, natural resources, transportation, and population movement are discussed here. One day, perhaps more, will be needed.
   d) Unit evaluation, pp. 43–44. One day.

B. *Major Problems, Questions, and Issues*: Listed here are some of the major problems and issues to which the Unit is devoted. This list is not intended to be complete, nor will every class face the same problems. They are listed here for consideration.

   1. A student must have a working knowledge of his textbook and the tool function it has. The questions, cartoons, time lines, illustrations, presidential information, dictionary of terms, index, bibliography, and special features such as the Declaration of Independence and the Constitution of the United States are items that will be used often.
   2. An appreciation of the changes in the American scene by comparing life in early colonial America with life in the United States is offered to the student.
   3. The permanence of change is made apparent to the student by contrasting changes in education, transportation, communication, manufacture, and government.
   4. The student should understand the three factors that influence growth . . . heredity, environment, and personal experience.
   5. The student is to grasp the study of history as a written record of change in man and his way of life.
   6. Geography is defined for the student as a description of the surface of the land.
   7. The effect of the Appalachian mountains on the westward migration is brought to the attention of the student.

8. Geographic conditions which led to sectional differences in the colonies should be understood.
9. The advantages of the natural highways west provided by the Piedmont river systems is important.
10. The natural passes through the Appalachian chain should be brought to the attention of the student.
11. The major landforms of the North American continent should be familiar to the student.
12. The effect of oceans, rivers, and lakes upon the growth of cities such as San Francisco, New Orleans, St. Louis, Kansas City, Minneapolis and St. Paul should be understood by the student.
13. The terms listed at the beginning of the Unit and the end of each chapter should be understood by the student before he attempts reading the material.
14. The geographic factors enabling the early settlers to spread quickly through the Central Plains area are important to the understanding of this unit.
15. The distinction between the Great Plains and the Central Plains is important for the student to make.

IV. Suggested Activities:
   A. *Introductory*:
      1. Films, filmstrips, etc. See the collective Bibliography.
      2. Displays of library books, book covers, samples of various map projections, etc.
      3. Samples of early maps showing perimeters lined with sea-serpents and evil demons of the unknown.
   B. *Developmental*:
      1. Research-type activities designed to acquaint students with atlases available in the school library and with what they contain.
      2. Student projects such as salt-soda maps.
      3. Creative expression through a written description of an airplane ride across the United States describing the seven natural regions from a bird's-eye view.
      4. Drill on states, cities, capitals, regions, rivers, lakes, gulfs, bays, and special geographic terms unfamiliar to the student.
      5. Appreciation-type activities having to do with local resources and history.
   C. *Culminating Activities*:
      1. Display student projects such as maps, charts, and other individual work.
      2. Review the material through the use of questions at the end of the unit or chapter.
      3. Testing.

V. Bibliographies:
   A. *Books*:
      1. Bakeless, Katherine and John, *They Saw America First*, Lippincott.

2. Duniosin, Roger, *They Put Out to Sea; the Story of the Map*, Knopf.
3. Langdon, William C., *Everyday Things in American Life*, Scribner.
4. Tannenbaum, Beulah and Sullman, Mya, *Understanding Maps; Charting the Land, Sea, and Sky*, Whittesey.

B. *Films*: These films are on hand at the Center for Audio-Visual Education.
1. C 7722 *Maps and Their Meaning*, 14 min.
2. C 7732 *Maps, Land Symbols and Terms*, 14 min.

C. *Filmstrips*: These Filmstrips are available at the Center for Audio-Visual Education.
1. FS 8892 *Age of Discovery and Exploration* (set of 7)
2. FS 2470 *Exploring Through Maps*
3. FS 7751 *Introduction to Maps* (set of 5)
4. FS 7272 *Maps and Their Meaning*
5. FS 8034 Map Series (2 fs)
6. FS 8882 *Starting With the Globe*

D. *Recordings*: These are available from the company at the listed address.
1. *The Growth of America Series*, 78rpm
Ideal Pictures Corporation
65 East South Water Street
Chicago 15, Ill.

E. *Others*: Many excellent student newspapers or magazines are available through the usual procurement channels. *Junior Review, Current Events*, and other such magazines are helpful in the current events program. There is a need for supplementing these student papers with the more sophisticated news media such as the daily paper or current news magazines such as *Time, Newsweek*, or other adult news digests. Students will need help interpreting the subtleties of adult news media. Television and radio coverage of major news items can be brought into the classroom or assigned for home viewing and listening.

VI. Suggested Evaluative Procedures:
A. *Teacher-Made Tests*: This is the major source of all evaluation in the classroom and probably the source best adapted to this unit. The objectives mentioned previously may be used as a starting point in the construction of these tests. The teacher-made test is apt to be the best coverage of the material covered in the class.
B. *Commercial Tests*: Many companies are engaged in the business of selling "standard" tests for use in American History courses. It is not possible to cover any given situation in a "company" test.
C. *Textbook Tests*: The teachers manual supplied with the present textbook offers a unit test at the close of each unit. The teacher may find this helpful in the construction of evaluative materials.

Evaluation of Learning

In our democratic society, the cultivation of the learning potential of each individual for useful citizenship is a major concern of teachers. In accepting this as our major goal we express our objectives in terms of behaviors to be learned which are consistent with this goal. The learning objectives of social studies classes are those understandings, attitudes, and skills which are likely to produce the desired behavior.

Evaluation is the means by which we determine the extent to which these objectives have been accomplished. It becomes the process by which the achievement of desired outcomes is observed and recorded, and the results of this process testify to the effectiveness of the teaching. Thus, broadly conceived, it is at the same time, indicative of the degree of student behavioral change and the success of the educational program itself.

Evaluation may be directed toward different objectives. It may be concerned with what an individual has learned, how groups of individuals of a special group—such as the academically gifted—have an identifiable talent for social leadership, or with the effects of experimentation or new types of organization and methodology. In whatever context used, however, evaluation has many aspects, amounts to considerably more than testing, and is a vital part of the teaching-learning situation in which the teacher is the central element.

The following guidelines are offered as a basis for a working philosophy of evaluation and measurement.

1. Evaluation should be carried on cooperatively. The teacher—with the help of students, other professional personnel, and parents—establishes goals, makes plans, and evaluates on this cooperative basis.

2. An effective program is continuous. It needs to be continuous because growth is continuous in a good educational program. It can proceed regularly through the use of some of the devices listed below, with more comprehensive methods used at the ends of units of work and before progress reports are made to parents.

3. It is comprehensive in nature. All phases and aspects of growth and development should be taken into account with provision for evaluating understandings, attitudes, and skills. Likewise, the instruments used should be comprehensive as to kind.

4. The process of measurement should be related directly to that of defining goals. The ends to be achieved must first be formulated; then measurement procedures can be sought as tools for appraising the extent to which the ends have been achieved.

5. Much of educational and psychological measurement is and probably will remain at a relatively low level of precision. In recognition of this, available procedures should be continued in use with the understanding that scores be treated as tentative hypotheses rather than as statistical absolutes.

6. The more elegant procedures of formal test and measurement should be supplemented by cruder procedures of informal observation, anecdotal description and rating, to obtain an assessment of the individual that is usefully complete and comprehensive.

7. No amount of ingenuity in developing improved procedures for measuring and appraising an individual will eliminate the need to interpret results in relation to the personality of that individual.

The following devices can be used to judge the extent and effectiveness of learning.

Check lists	Cumulative records
Rating scales	Anecdotal records
Group-made tests	Teacher-made tests
Diaries or logs	Standardized tests
Graphs of individual progress	Profiles
	Case studies
Samples of work	Scrapbooks
Group discussions and interviews	Sociometric tests
	Autobiographies
Behavior records	Photographs of
Questionnaires	displays or activities
Informal observation	

Summary Comments—8th-Grade American History Unit

Even though the activities and experiences for this unit are not spelled out specifically, the opportunities for pupil-teacher planning, small and large group activity, and individualized study are obvious. It must be kept in mind that the unit is simply a guide for the teacher and his students. Possibilities for utilization of the core concept are unlimited. The philosophy and enthusiasm of each teacher will determine the effectiveness of the program.

Extensive use of appropriate audio-visual aids, including television, will enhance perception of concepts to be learned. Films, filmstrips, and television activities may be of considerable value to the slower learners and/or remedial readers. Student projects, research-type activities, reading *Time* and *Newsweek*, (all suggested in the unit plan) will motivate the more able and ambitious pupils and strengthen the program in terms of meeting individual needs and differences. Continuous evaluation by teachers, pupils, and coordinators will improve the teaching-learning process. Each individual within these groups will consider himself a member of the team, and will be motivated to do his part in a more professional and interesting fashion in the future.

Articulation—Grades 7, 8, and 9

Examination of content for the 7th and 8th grades may suggest a subtle "spiraling" approach to content in grades 7, 8, and 9. An examination of cultures and contributions of major nations of the world in grade 7 would lead to opportunities for comparisons with American culture in the 8th grade. Major emphasis placed upon geographical features of important nations of the world in grade 7 will set the stage for generalizations to be sought regarding the effects of geographical features in the United States. Exploration and development of the United States were influenced by geographic features in much the same way as these features influenced other major nations of the world. The alert teacher can motivate reflective thinking along the lines of "structure" rather than "facts-to-be-learned," thereby facilitating student thinking in terms of how the 7th-grade unit provides a basis for the 8th-grade social content.

The relationship of subject matter in 8th grade will often be reflected upon during the study of civics and world history in the 9th grade. Exploration of the economic system and state history will harken back to exploration and development of America. Personal-social understandings of occupations, the home, and other social institutions (content by grade 9 civics) will be more easily understood and mastered by students as a result of having been exposed to the 8th-grade social studies curriculum. The world history unit at the 9th-grade level will be strengthened by earlier concepts based upon cultures of major nations of the world during 7th grade.

Chapter 6

The Setauket Junior High
School Social Studies Program

For Grades 7 Through 9, Setauket, L. I., N. Y.*

The Challenge

Grading has been the traditional way of organizing schools for the vertical progression of students for over a century. In 1848, when the graded structure was introduced in this country, people believed that the needs of society and of the learner could be served by a rather simple program of elementary education. Obviously, knowledge and skills available to the learner, and needed by him, were more limited than they are today. The graded school is based upon three assumptions: (1) elementary and secondary schools should "cover" a specific amount of subject matter; (2) the subject matter should be identified and rigorously prescribed; and (3) individual differences merely determine the student's chances of success to cover the prescribed material.[1]

Many in Setauket were aware of the fact that the graded system was not providing the type of organization that was consistent with our philosophy. The assumptions made by the National Committee for the Project on Instruction exemplify our thoughts concerning individual differences and school organization. These assumptions are:

The instructional program of the school should be designed to develop the potentialities of all members of the school population, as individuals and as members of society.

The instructional program should include the learning of basic generalizations and the development of ways of knowing and thinking.

The vertical pattern of school organization should provide for the continuous, unbroken, upward progression of all learners, with due regard for the great range of differences among and within them.[2]

The concept of nongrading seemed the most logical to implement our philosophy, aims, and objectives. The nongraded school is characterized by primary concern for the individual and all individuals. This point of view did not overlook the place of subject matter. Knowledge and skills are necessary for developing the maximum potential of all learners.

Several of the advantages of nongrading and problems related to making appropriate changes in points of view, program, and structure, were pointed out by Goodlad. He said:

Nongrading sweeps away the graded superstructure, graded content, graded textbooks, graded normative standards, graded children, graded teachers, graded expectations, and graded nomenclature to which we have long been accustomed. It is the fact that we have been so long accustomed to these accoutrements of graded schools that we fear and resist their departure. For them, nongrading substitutes continuous pupil progress uninhibited by grade barriers; subject-matter organized sequentially around fundamental concepts, principles, and generalizations; instructional materials gathered together for the task at hand and the varying abilities of the learners involved with it; criterion performance standards inherent in the learning task itself (excellence is determined from actual performance, not

---

* Information supplied by Richard Dawe, Chairman of Social Studies Department, Setauket Junior High School, Setauket, Long Island, New York.

[1] See *Schools for the 60's,* a report of the NEA Project on Instruction for discussion of nongrading, multigrading and grading. New York: McGraw-Hill Book Co., 1963, pp. 79–80.

[2] *Ibid.,* p. 79.

comparisons with others); alternative classroom placements for learners based on pupil diagnoses; individual expectations for students; and still other provisions.[3]

In addition to vertical organization considerations, we were concerned about horizontal structure. It was necessary to provide a better system for dividing a given student population into instructional groups and allocating these students to teachers. The explanation of how this was achieved is explained in the next section.

Cooperative Planning in Social Studies

The *Cycle* curriculum in social studies was developed as part of a school-wide program. Dr. Paul Gelinas, supervising principal, Mr. Aime Lacoste, junior high school principal, and the chairmen of the departments started working on this system in 1955.

At that time, the "track" system had become popular throughout the United States. An investigation of this system was conducted and, although we felt it had many advantages, the following drawbacks were noted:

1. Students were grouped by general ability and were in the same track for all subjects. This ignores the fact that many students do better in some subjects than in others.
2. Once a student was classified in a track, movement to another track became difficult, if not impossible.
3. The strongest objections to tracking were psychological. It has been argued that a stigma is placed on the lowest track student and that the highest track student tends to develop undesirable attitudes.

We[4] felt that these disadvantages were so important that unless they could be overcome, homogeneous grouping would not be used. An attempt was made to devise a system which would provide the benefits of tracking and eliminate the disadvantages. The result was the cycle system. Although the basic approach was identical, each department had to devise its own program because of the difference in material.

The objectives of the Social Studies Department at Setauket were considered as basic for change.

---

[3] Goodlad, John I., O'Toole, John F., Jr., and Tyler, Louise L., *Computers and Information Systems in Education.* New York: Harcourt, Brace and World, Inc., 1966, p. 16.

[4] Information supplied by Richard Dawe, Chairman of the Social Studies Department, Setauket, L. I., N. Y.

These are: 1. to stimulate a curiosity for and understanding of the study of man and his institutions; 2. to develop an understanding of the individual's place in society; 3. to encourage active participation and leadership in our society; and 4. to start students on careers in the social studies field.

The horizontal organization was devised with these two basic concepts: (1) that students should be grouped homogeneously, by subject; and (2) that students should be able to progress at individual rates. The social studies program was developed by the staff and coordinated by the administration. A separate curriculum for each of the five social studies levels was written.

Students are selected for the various groups on the basis of scores received on standardized social studies achievement tests, class marks in Grade 6 Social Studies, and teacher recommendations. Students can, and are, moved from group to group during the school year at any time their achievement warrants it.

There are five homogeneous groupings in social studies. With this kind of system, it is imperative that material be available on different levels. A great variety of enrichment materials are also needed. At least five different textbooks are available for each subject taught. They vary in difficulty, with the top section using senior high school texts. In addition to the texts, other materials are available. They include records, filmstrips, films, tapes, and slides. Individual projects and research are encouraged. To this end, a close liaison is maintained with the library. In the last two years, original source readings have been utilized with all groups.

Conferences

Frequent conferences are held by the department chairman and the teachers. During these meetings student progress is discussed. An evaluation of individual students is made. Where satisfactory progress is noted, students are moved to the next cycle. However, this is never done without a prior student-teacher conference. At these conferences students are advised of the challenge in the new cycle and recommendations are made in order to prepare the student. The teacher may suggest a change in study habits or give the student a list of readings. Most important, the student is made aware of just what will be expected of him.

When unsatisfactory progress is observed, the teacher and department head attempt to evaluate the problem. A program is developed to help the student overcome his difficulty. Although this program is outlined in the department head-teacher conference, it is finalized during a student-teacher conference. These programs vary depending upon the student but often include (1) parent conferences; (2) special help classes; (3) tutoring; (4) placement in a lower step; (5) individual projects and research; (6) guidance conferences; and (7) organization of study habits.

By using this conference approach continual contact is maintained with all students.

The main function of the Department Chairman is to act as guidance or placement counselor in the social studies. Almost daily, students are evaluated and conferences held. Students' progress is discussed and changes made. The teachers also hold individual student conferences regularly. There is a teacher-chairman conference weekly. These conferences are necessary because of the close observation which must be kept on an individual student's progress.

This program has been in operation for more than 10 years. Plans have now been made to extend it into our high school.[5]

The provisions for meeting individual needs and individual differences are outstanding features of the Setauket Social Studies Program. Educators have not all agreed upon precise methods of teaching or upon one precise way in which individuals learn. Much research is still required as related to the learning process. However, regardless of what theory or combinations of theories one may subscribe to, there are many points in which all theorists agree. Important among these are the recognition that all learners do not need to engage in the same activity in order to achieve recognized goals and that individual motivation does have influence on the degree of learning, especially when that motivation is strengthened by successful experience. Guidance of the learner is essential through his junior high years in helping him to accept himself, to set appropriate goals for himself, and to be able to evaluate his successes and failures unemotionally.

The features of flexible homogeneous grouping, a great variety of teaching materials, extensive use of appropriate audio-visual aids, individual projects and research activities, regular evaluations and/or conferences with students, and a guidance-oriented approach in the Setauket plan exemplify these common principles to a high degree.

Social Studies in New York State

Since the curriculum for Steps 1–5 is based upon the New York State Department of Education curriculum, it seemed appropriate to relate suggestions and guidelines as outlined by the State Department of Education. Hopefully, the reader can gain greater insight into the program and better appreciate the common philosophy underlying its content and organization.

All aspects of the school program can potentially contribute to responsible citizenship and to democratic living. In a more limited sense, the term "citizenship studies" is used to designate that area of the curriculum which concerns the conditions in which man lives and works, the origins, patterns and problems of American society, and the opportunities available to, and the responsibilities incumbent upon, those who live in it. The emphasis in this area is upon understanding man's relation to man and the individual's relation to various groups.[6]

The significance of the area of citizenship studies is defined as follows:

The citizenship studies are at the heart of the cultural heritage and incorporate the very bases of the democratic way of life in the United States. Upon a knowledge of his country, especially of the values and motivations of its people, the young adolescent intensifies his patriotic sentiment. From the lives of national heroes he is helped to develop his ideals; from the contributions of leaders in the political and economic life of the present and past he begins to develop a concept of roles in adult society. Through these studies the pupil becomes conscious of the rapid changes characteristic of our era and of the problems confronting individuals and nations. The young adolescent becomes oriented more toward other people; through the study of human problems he gains an understanding of values and motives as they have operated in the past and as they are evidenced in the world of today; and he gains a clearer understanding of his own feelings, desires, and relationships with others. He gains, too, some understanding of the economic realities of life, so necessary in appraising himself in relation to the role he is soon to assume. Treating history as a story, with emphasis upon the romantic and adventurous aspects, capitalizes interests which are strong at the early secondary level.[7]

Noteworthy emphases in practice are enumerated as follows:

1. Learnings in this area are constantly related to current affairs and contemporary life.

---

[5] Ibid.

[6] The University of the State of New York, A Design for Early Secondary Education in New York State. Albany: The State Education Department, 1954, p. 46.

[7] Ibid., p. 47.

2. Facts are utilized primarily for the development of concepts and attitudes which in turn form a framework for later understanding of and dealing with civic, economic, and social problems.

3. Opportunity is provided for helping pupils gain experience in using an intelligent approach to problem solving in economic, civic, and social areas.

4. Many mediums of mass communication are utilized in studying current affairs.

5. When controversial issues are studied, pupils are helped to examine as fully as possible all sides of a question.

6. Pupils are helped to understand the relation between the work in citizenship studies classes and experiences in citizenship elsewhere in the program of the school.

7. Advantage is taken of the fact that the content of the citizenship studies area lends itself particularly well to pupil participation in planning and carrying on learning activities.

8. Community resources are extensively utilized in connection with citizenship studies.[8]

The Social Studies Cycle

Completes

Step
1 Minimum required courses without State Regents Examination
2 Minimum required coures with State Regents Examinations plus ½ year elective
3 Minimum required courses plus 1 year of electives

[8] *Ibid.*, pp. 47–48.

4 Minimum required courses plus second year of American History
5 Minimum required courses plus second year of American History electives (College Course)
6 Same as Step 5 plus independent study

Required State Minimums in Junior and Senior High School Social Studies

1 The Community and the State
2 United States History
3 The Economic World (or similar "World" course)
4 World History*
5 American History* (1 year course)
or
American History* (2 year course)

Descriptions of Social Studies Courses by Levels

Social Studies 1

This class completes the minimum social studies curriculum prescribed by the New York State Board of Regents. Courses include New York State and American history, geography, and government, as well as 9th grade world economic geography.

A median class score of 50th percentile on nationally standardized achievement tests is typical for this group.

Social Studies 2

This class completes the social studies curriculum prescribed by the New York State Board of Regents.

* State Regents Examinations

THE SOCIAL STUDIES CYCLE

	CYCLE I (Gr. 7–8)		CYCLE II (Gr. 8–9)		CYCLE III (Gr. 9–10)
Step	*Course*	*Step*	*Course*	*Step*	*Course*
1	The Community and the State	1	New York State's Role in the Growth of Our Nation	1	New York State's Role in the World Community
2	History of New York State	2	New York in American History	2	New York: World Economic Center
3	New York in Colonial America	3	Contributions of New York to American Traditions	3	The Relationship of American and World Cultures
4	New York and the United States to the Revolution	4	The United States and the Old World	4	Modern Civilization
5	New York and the United States to the Civil War	5	The United States and the Modern World	5	World History*
6	Independent Study	6	Independent Study	6	Independent Study

MOBILITY	*MOBILITY*	*MOBILITY*
Any student can move to any step except near the end of the cycle.	Any student can move down. Only restriction up is near the end of the cycle.	Any student can move down. Only restriction up is into Step 5.

Courses include New York State and American history, geography, and government, as well as 9th grade world economic geography.

A median class score of 75th percentile on nationally standardized achievement tests is typical for this group.

Social Studies 3

The achievement level of this class approximates one-quarter year in advance of the curriculum prescribed by the New York State Board of Regents. Enrichment instruction emphasizes the interrelationship of New York State to American history and subsequently to world economic geography and history.

A median class score of 80th percentile on nationally standardized achievement tests is typical for this group.

Social Studies 4

The achievement level of this class is one-half year in advance of the curriculum prescribed by the New York State Board of Regents. Enrichment instruction emphasizes the interrelationship of New York State to American history and subsequently to world economic geography and history.

A median class score of 90th percentile on nationally standardized achievement tests is typical for this group.

Social Studies 5

The achievement level of this class is one full year in advance of the curriculum prescribed by the New York State Board of Regents. Three years of work will be completed in the first two years of junior high school. Courses in New York State and American history, geography, and government, as well as world economic geography are included in this program. During the third year of junior high, an intensive world history course is given. This program grants two high school credits for completion of grades 9 and 10 social studies.

A median class score of over 95th percentile on nationally standardized tests is typical for this group.

Conclusion

The content for the social studies for the 7th, 8th, and 9th grades is consistent with the "widening horizons" concept. Step 1, in 7th grade, relates to the community and the state. Finally, Step 5, in 9th grade, is concerned with world history. In effect, this approach is from the "concrete" to the "abstract." Analysis of the culture and society of the community and the state will point to problems and similarities in other cultures throughout the world. The widening horizon plan may help to alleviate degrees of provincialism and ethnocentricity that are either unwise or unhealthful. Methods using tapes, various source material, and extensive use of films can lead to greater appreciation of one's own culture and an understanding of other cultures in the world in which we live.

While continuous evaluation of pupil progress is an essential part of this program, there is reliance upon the use of the New York Regents Examination as an indication of pupil progress.

Chapter 7

The Social Studies Program at University School

Southern Illinois University, Carbondale, Illinois

Mabel Lane Bartlett
Associate Professor of Education and Supervisor of Student Teaching
University School, College of Education
Southern Illinois University

Development of Social Studies Curriculum at University School

At University School in 1952, a Social Studies Curriculum Committee was chosen to evaluate and recommend a plan for a social studies program for the entire school, including pre-kindergarten through grade 12. By the spring of 1954, a general outline of a social studies program had been developed, presented, and accepted by the entire University School faculty.

In the fall of 1954 the Social Studies Curriculum Committee was enlarged, reorganized, and began work toward more detailed plans. The membership of the Committee included the school librarian; three faculty representatives from the elementary grades; three faculty members from the senior high school; and two parents of students in University School. Dr. Clarence Samford, S. I. U. Professor and specialist in Social Studies, served as consultant to the Committee.

From the outset, the Committee agreed that the general objective of the Social Studies program should be to help the student develop as a social being and that in order to serve the needs and best interests of the students, the program needed to be pupil-centered. It was felt that the program should start with the young pupil in his local environment and expand into community, state, nation, and world as he proceeded through the various grades. As the program developed, the Committee was careful that it would be in harmony with the over-all philosophy and objectives

of University School; that it should provide for flexibility, yet establish general topics or areas of work for each grade level; that it should avoid undesirable or unnecessary repetition of subject matter areas; that it should include a wide coverage of subject matter; and that it should serve as a guide for teacher and student teacher planning.

Philosophy and Objectives of University School

The following Philosophy and Objectives, presented by the General Curriculum Committee in January, 1951, were approved by the Parent-Teacher Association and remain the present guide at University School.

Philosophy

Education should seek to develop to the fullest the capacities of the individual as a human personality and to prepare him for effective participation in a democratic world whose aim it is to do the most good for the most people. Education, therefore, should encourage the mastery of such knowledge, the acquisition of such attitudes, and the development of such habits and skills as will make it possible for the learner to follow the most desirable way of living.

Objectives

1. To help each individual discover and develop his potentialities for happy and successful living.
2. To develop in each individual habits of self-reliance, self-discipline, and resourcefulness in using leisure time worthily and in meeting other everyday situations satisfactorily.
3. To develop in each individual the desire and

ability to think, to read and listen with understanding.

4. To develop in each individual the desire and ability to speak and write effectively.
5. To develop in each individual desirable attitudes and practices concerning health, physical fitness, and safety.
6. To develop in each individual his abilities to understand and enjoy beauty in literature, art, music, and nature.
7. To develop in each individual the ability to know how to purchase and use goods and services intelligently.
8. To develop in each individual the desire and ability to understand the rights and duties of the citizen of a democratic society and to perform his obligations as a member of the community, of the state, of the nation, and of the world.
9. To develop in each individual the desire to respect other persons regardless of age, creed, or race.
10. To develop in each individual proper attitudes concerning the significance of the family for the individual and society, and an understanding of the conditions conducive to successful family life.
11. To develop in each individual skills, understanding and attitudes that will make him an intelligent and productive participant in economic life.

General Objectives of the Social Studies Curriculum of University School

Following a thorough study of findings concerning the teaching of social studies, and consideration of the objectives of several other social studies programs, the Committee developed the following statement of general objectives for the social studies program of University School:

The objectives of the social studies program should be toward continuous behavioral change in the direction of:

1. Assuming social and civic responsibility based on knowledge and appreciation of duties, rights, and responsibilities of citizens.
2. Increasingly acquiring information as a basis for critical judgment.
3. Skillfully securing, sifting, evaluating, organizing, and presenting information.
4. Continuously using knowledge and appreciation of the past as background for the present.
5. Attempting to understand the interdependence of all peoples and all groups and the necessity for cooperation.
6. Developing a love for our country in the form of an intelligent patriotism.

Grade Placement Themes

Grade placement of subject matter in the social studies areas was given careful consideration by

the Committee. It was agreed that grade placement and theme should be based upon the needs and interests of each particular age group as well as upon the needs of our society as a whole. The following themes proceed from the immediate and known environment to those more remote and unknown and were chosen with the hope that they would unify the program and generally determine the scope of the work in each grade or course:

Grade Level	Theme
Pre-Kindergarten and Kindergarten	New People and Places
Grade 1	School and Home
Grade 2	Our Neighborhood and Community
Grade 3	Carbondale and Neighboring Communities
Grade 4	Early Civilizations
Grade 5	The United States
Grade 6	Our American Neighbors
Grade 7	Our World Neighbors in Europe, Asia, Africa, Australia
Grade 8	Our Democracy, the United States
Grade 9–10	World History 1 Unit
Grade 10–11	World Geography ½ Unit
Grade 11	American History 1 Unit
Grade 11–12	Civics ½ Unit
Grade 11–12	Social and Political Problems 1 Unit
Grade 11–12	Economics ½ Unit

Library Instruction

Although a program for library instruction was detailed in the Language Arts Curriculum Guide, it was recognized that social studies affords numerous opportunities for library use. Plans were made for the librarian to work with the classroom teacher to help plan, compile, and provide special instruction in the finding and use of library materials and skills needed at the various grade levels.

Placed at the end of each course outline was a list of library tools, special reference books, and indexes, pertaining to the particular theme.

Current Events

The Committee felt that current events should be an essential part of any social studies program and should have a place at every grade level. The *what*, *when*, and *how* were left to the discretion of the teacher.

Suggested Topics for Grades 7 and 8

The following broad topics were suggested within the themes of the 7th and the 8th grades. The list was to be considered as a guide and was subject to modification or substitution at the discretion of the teacher.

Grade 7 Topics

Theme—Our World Neighbors in Europe, Asia, Africa, and Australia
    Units of Study
        1. Our Wonderful World
        2. Egypt—The Cradle of Civilization
        3. Greece—Its Glorious Past
        4. The Romans—Their Contributions
        5. The Story of Civilization in Central Europe During the Middle Ages
        6. Our Inheritance from the British Isles
        7. The U.S.S.R., The World's Largest Nation
        8. Asia
        9. Africa
        10. Australia and New Zealand

Grade 8 Topics

Theme—Our Democracy, the United States
    Units of Study
        1. Use of Geographical Tools: Globe, Projections, Atlas
        2. History and Geography of the United States
        3. Our National Government: Its Structure and Development
        4. Illinois: History, Government, Geography
        5. The Flag: Its History, Display, and Use
        6. Conservation of Natural and Human Resources (if time allows)

Four Friends from Faraway Places[1]

7th Grade, University School
Time: Five Weeks

Who wears a Sari? Who is Dr. Azikiwe? What is the chief use of peanut oil? Where is the Inland Sea? What is saffron? Questions! Questions! For five busy weeks.

Unfamiliar terms: Ibo, paddy, baht, ghat. Faraway places: Gulf of Guinea, Lagos, Hyderabad, Siam. Strange-sounding names: Fulani, Shikoku, Buddha, Ganges.

But at University School in Carbondale, the myriad questions now have answers; the new terms have taken on meaning; and the strange names have been identified. This came about through a multitude of activities climaxed with visits from four foreign-born persons who were living in the community.

The five-week activities described below were

not only a highlight early in the second semester's work but set a pattern for work later in the year, using additional foreign friends to bring reality to a study of other faraway lands.

At University School, as in many others, the central theme of the 7th-grade social studies program is the Old World: Europe, Asia, Africa, Australia. The social studies-language arts instructional period is a daily two-hour block of time.

How to motivate social-studies learning and to enhance its significance continuously challenges the teacher in that field. The success of this particular project seemed due in part to thorough pre-planning by the teacher with provisions for flexibility largely pupil-planned and peer-disciplined, along with being "sparked" by the contest idea; it served to direct the group's ultimate efforts to high standards. The teacher's role then became that of director and guide.

Nowadays, almost every community has persons with first-hand knowledge of foreign lands. The individual teacher can acquaint herself with such persons and determine their possible contribution to the social studies program.

Class Organization for Work

The organization of the class into four committees, each with a different country to study and present facts about, provided not only the motivation of small-group activity and the chance for competition with other groups, but it also provided chances for the pupils to learn in first-hand activity the techniques of group work. The following is a list of Committee Work Suggestions adapted as a guide for work on the committees.

Committee Work Suggestions

Duties of Committee Chairman
    Help organize work
    Give ideas
    Listen to ideas
    Coordinate work
    Report on progress
    Ask for help
    Lead discussion
    Introduce topic
    Introduce speaker

Responsibilities of Other Committee Members
    Give ideas
    Cooperate with others
    Be prompt with work
    Really work

Standards for Presenting Findings
    Know the material
    Make it interesting

---

[1] Permission to adapt from "Five Friends from Faraway Places," *Illinois Education*, March, 1959, granted by Illinois Education Association.

Have necessary materials ready
Give clear demonstrations
Present facts in order
Speak distinctly
Define new terms

Day-by-day and week-by-week activities are given on pages 58 and 59.

The Contest

To the pupils, one of the major features of the unit was the contest. It was suggested and organized during the introductory days of the unit. Contest points were given for the following projects related to the work underway:

1. *Vocabulary* Any pertinent new word defined and used in explanatory way (1 each)
2. *Spelling* Three 20-word lists (1 each)
3. *Clippings* From current sources, for posting (1 each)
4. *Maps* (Given letter grade by sub-committee)
   A=3   C=1
   B=2   D=0
5. *Exhibits* Labelled and displayed (1 each)
6. *Facts* (2 each)
   The fact
   Title or source
   Author or vol. no.
   Page no.
   Your name and group no.
   Dates
7. *Outline on Whole Country* (Given letter grade by teacher)
   A=10   C=5
   B=8   D=2
8. *Written Report on Specific Topic* (Given letter grade by teacher)
   A=10   C=5
   B=8   D=2
9. *Guests* Invited adults who attended committee report (10 each)

A four-member sub-committee, composed of one pupil from each committee or team, graded or scored most of the contest entries. With the exception of the group chairman and secretary, who had many planning and recording responsibilities, each pupil represented his team or committee on some sub-committee.

1. *Vocabulary*

New Words and unusual terms were submitted for "Vocabulary" scoring. Such were watched for as the unit progressed. The new word or phrase was listed, defined clearly, and used in a well-worded sentence. There was no limit on the number of new words which could be submitted at the three specified times during the contest.

2. *Spelling*

Spelling also counted on the contest. A spelling list of the following 60 words was compiled.

banana	amount	address
cocoa	stomach	they're
coffee	telephone	two
dollar	animal	earth
their	tobacco	geography
friend	except	government
entertainment	writing	written
beginning	difference	business
elephant	accept	health
to	holiday	sincerely
occurrence	there	island
describe	too	acquaint
picture	description	library
pitcher	piece	boundary
your	decision	mischievous
peace	you're	language
physical	probably	listen
poison	athletic	ocean
sailor	example	neighbor
scale	explain	mountain

The words were selected for appropriateness and usefulness. Words pertaining to the unit were selected from the Dolch list of 2,000 most commonly written words. The list was divided into three 20-word tests. All lists were then copied by each pupil with attention given to pronunciation, meaning, spelling, and legibility. The Day-By-Day Activities Chart will indicate when regular study and review time was provided.

3. *Clippings*

Clippings from any current sources about any of the countries being studied could be submitted to the clippings sub-committee for counting and posting. The bulletin board was continuously changing. Name, team number, source, and date were required on each entry. Other sources included books, pamphlets, and many materials which were excellent sources for information but could not be cut or marked in any way. These were shown and briefly discussed at the beginning of each day, then placed in a central place for common use. The clippings sub-committee kept accurate scores on these contributions.

4. *Maps*

Maps of many kinds, sizes, materials and topics were submitted to the maps sub-committee for appraisal and accreditation for the contest. Several of these maps were used in the oral reporting to guests.

CHART OF DAY-BY-DAY ACTIVITIES

	Monday	Tuesday
FEBRUARY 10	General introduction to entire unit. Countries which might be studied: foreign students available, time limitations, methods of presentation, etc. Explain contest. Select committees and countries. Copy spelling lists. Group planning.	Outlines out and explained. Directed notetaking, using text and room encyclopedias. Trip to library for general instructions on where and how to find materials. Further group planning. Pronounce spelling list #1 noting tricky parts.
FEBRUARY 17	Pronounce spelling list #2. Committees meet for necessary group work before individuals work on specific subjects in room or in library. Teacher circulates to give help, encourage, and note progress in preparation by individuals.	Study spelling in small groups. Progress report #2 (written, including individual report of additional facts, ideas, or plans). Discuss use, form, and progress on outline. Committees meet to continue work as a group or on individual work—in room or in library.
FEBRUARY 24	Take and score pre-test on spelling list #3. Progress report #3. Develop and write group standards for oral reports (two pupils prepare a poster clearly stating these standards). Remind class that completed outlines should be submitted next day. Committees meet.	Study spelling list #3. Completed outlines due. Committees meet. Continue work in groups or as individuals. Teacher, chairman, and secretaries confirm speaking times with foreign students and arrange for their transportation, if needed.
MARCH 2	Committee #1 report on *India*, 1st hour; pupils present information. 2nd hour, talk by foreign student from India with parents of committee members as guests for both hours. Note: Only the members of the reporting committee were allowed in the classroom for the noon-hour preparation preceding their report.	Appraise unit as a whole so far. Also point out good points of 1st committee's report referring to the listening chart prepared earlier in group work. Review contest as it now stands. While committee #1 work on contest entries, committees #2, #3, #4 meet.
MARCH 9	Committee #4 report on *Japan*. Followed by talk by Japanese student.	Again appraise our unit using the group plan to review the various activities. Plan test: 5-part, pupil and teacher-made objective test covering facts presented. Write a thank-you note to each foreign speaker, each note signed by each of the 23 pupils in class.

Four Foreign Friends
7th Grade Social Studies—Language Arts   1:00 and 2:00

Wednesday	Thursday	Friday
Leaders and secretaries write invitations to selected foreign students. Review outline-making and note-taking. Continue notes on country in general. Review requirements for "Facts" for "Fact Box." Practice on spelling, helping one another in pairs.	Work again on spelling list #1. Progress Report #1 (individual, written summarizing facts found and making suggestions for group report). Teacher check on progress on completing outline of facts on whole country. Group discussion about characteristics of a good report. Committee meetings to select specific topics for final report.	Contest maps shown then submitted to appropriate sub-committee. Vocabulary #1 submitted (a few sample entries read). Spelling test #1 taken and collected for sub-committee grading. Sub-committees meet to check contest submissions for week #1. Contest report. Committees meet.
Take, then self-check trial test on spelling list #2. Each committee make progress report to teacher, privately, on anticipated plans. (Most committees want an element of surprise in their presentation.) Individuals or committees continue preparations.	Additional maps accepted. Vocabulary #2 submitted. Spelling test #2 taken. Sub-committees meet. Contest report for week #2. Check again on work on outlines. Committees meet.	No School.
Teacher returns outlines and reviews University School Style Sheet for Written Work, then helps pupils begin first draft of written report (on topic selected, using appropriate portion of outline, and own notes). Committees meet, if needed, or individuals continue on work.	Study spelling list #3. Conclude work on written report following University School Style Sheet for Written Work. Committees meet. Complete plans for next week's reports before guests. Group discussion of our individual responsibilities as representatives of our country, review appropriate courtesies to our guests, and answer questions or make recommendations about plans.	Spelling test #3. Vocabulary #3 accepted. More maps accepted. Final draft of written reports finished and turned in. Sub-committees meet. Contest report for week #3. Committee meetings for last minute review of report plans, including manner of introducing speaker, seating of guests, arrangement of room. (Noon hour of "day" reserved for scheduled committee.)
Committee #2 report on *Southeast Asia*. Followed by introduction of and talk by foreign student-guest. Parents of Committee #2 as guests this day. Note: Each foreign student came in his native costume, brought objects to show, records to play, sang or danced, etc.	Committee #3 report on *Nigeria*. Followed by talk by Nigerian student. Parents of Committee members as guests. Note: Each day, the committee in charge could rearrange and decorate the classroom as they chose.	Last day for submitting maps and vocabulary for contest. Committee #4 meet, if needed. Sub-committees meet. Contest report for week #4.
Open "Fact Box," distribute "Facts" to pupils' desks for checking and sorting for team credit. Tally "Fact" scores. Conclude contest; winners distribute the accumulated written materials for notebook compilation; losers plan party.	Take test covering chiefly facts, attitudes, and learnings from the reports given or heard. Distribute any remaining written work done during entire unit. Organize and compile into notebook form.	Return test and discuss its value. Appraise unit, week-by-week. Enjoy a short, room party planned and given in the classroom by the losers in the contest.

5. *Exhibits*

Exhibits also counted. They could be any artifact from one of the four countries. Each exhibit was to be labelled for sharing in the room.

6. *Facts*

Facts slipped into the sealed "Fact Box" were the last contest item checked. Facts were to be well written and clearly stated in complete sentences. They could pertain to any one of the countries being studied. Each fact was to be authenticated with data about its source, title, author or volume, publisher, publication date, page reference.

The acquired information was then organized into outline form. The following outline was given as a guide for organizing information about the various countries:

    I. Natural Features
      A. Boundaries
      B. Size
        1. Area
        2. Extent
      C. Climate
        1. Rainfall
        2. Temperature
      D. Waterways and Lakes
      E. Surface
      F. Plant and Animal Life
   II. History and Government
      A. Historical Sketch
        1. Early Inhabitants
        2. Growth and Development
      B. Government
        1. Political Divisions
        2. Types of Government
          a. National
          b. Local
        3. Leaders and Ideals
      C. Population
  III. Economics
      A. Resources
      B. Products
      C. Industries
      D. Domestic and Foreign Trade
      E. Transportation and Communication
      F. Money, Weights, Measures
  IV. Social Development
      A. Major Religions
      B. Education
      C. National or Local Customs
      D. Health and welfare
   V. Cultural Achievements
      A. Music
      B. Literature
      C. Language
      D. Arts
      E. Architecture
  VI. Cities
      A. Location
      B. Population

7. *Outline on Whole Country*

The notes compiled during the search for information were cumulative, written according to the suggestions in our language book, and finally organized into the outline from which the written and oral reports were made. Notes were numbered consecutively as taken from various sources. Source information—such as title, author, publishers, etc.—was given in the margin.

These rules were followed in preparing the outlines:

Number each main topic with Roman Numerals followed by a period.
Indent each subtopic under its main topic.
Indent details under their subtopics.
Begin each main topic, each subtopic, and each detail with a capital letter.
Arrange numbers and letters in columns so that each column forms a straight line.

Each committee member had all six of the general topics of the outline to develop on his committee's country, following the rules for outlining as given above.

8. *Written Report*

Portions of the outlines were used as a guide for the only required written report turned in in advance of presenting the oral reports. The following rules were set up to be followed in the preparation of their written report:

Use standard size (8½ by 11 inches) lined paper. Write on one side of the paper only.
Write in black, blue, or blue-black ink. Use either a fountain or a ballpoint pen.
Use the line for the margin at the left. Provide a half-inch margin at the right of the paper.
Indent paragraphs uniformly one inch.
Write the date in the upper left corner of the paper. Write name in natural order in the upper right corner.
Center the title on the top line of the first page only. Number succeeding pages in the upper right corner.
Leave a blank line between the title and the composition.
Write clearly and neatly. Make the general appearance of the paper as attractive as possible.

9. *Guests*

Each "Guest" counted 10 points. Parents were invited to visit on the day of their child's report. Other guests could also be invited by the individual pupils to hear his committee report. Upon arrival guests were greeted by some member of the committee and escorted to a place in the classroom. Ten or 12 guests could be seated without over-crowding, yet retain the intimacy of the class-room. Although teenagers do not always welcome parent visitation, the contest points caused the pupils to "encourage" their parents to visit.

10. *Oral Report*

In this unit the oral report was not considered for a contest score, but might very well have been used. An oral report was given by each pupil along with those of other members of his committee. Each committee's method of presentation was developed by its members with the approval of the teacher. Creativeness was evidenced in the committees' skits, dramatizations, use of maps, reports, quiz programs, demonstrations, use of films. Criteria for these reports included speaking distinctly, knowing the material, having the presentation organized, making it interesting, looking at the audience, and using notes sparingly.

The following list gives several activities which were considered by the various committees for use in helping them in presenting their facts in an interesting, effective way:

    Preview, select, and use films
    Give dramatizations
    Take trips
    Draw on art activities
    Prepare and use graphs or charts
    Give a quiz
    Speaker
    Prepare an exhibit
    Select and use recordings and other music
    Present folk lore or folk dancing
    Use opaque projector or other mechanical aid

Group-Determined Regulations

Room-rules developed by the group served as standards for self-control throughout the five weeks of the unit. Possible "deducts" to be taken from an individual's contest scores held infractions to a minimum. Rules were to make suggestions, bring materials, remember others' rights, do your share, to be a polite listener, speak distinctly, attend to business, have materials ready, move about quietly, leave things in order, and be prompt.

Plans for Pupil Appraisal

Three spaced progress reports, timely and concise, served to summarize progress and focus on the ultimate goal: an interesting, informative committee report. Progress reports gave information of various kinds: the country of origin of the committee's guest, the guest's name, date he would visit the class, some of the facts the committee

planned to explore, and suggested ways for presentation.

Conclusion

The unit had a number of strong points. The objective, international understanding, was timely and built on an existing interest in foreigners. Over-all plans were balanced and flexible, and included varied activities. Subject-matter lines were unimportant. Both planning and evaluation were cooperative and continuous. Many socially desirable activities were possible. Adolescent peer-interests were followed. Goals, responsibilities, and standards of behavior were cooperatively developed and clearly stated. Every child was involved, but conformity and individuality had their places. Required skills were within the learners' competences, and problems were within their comprehension. Individual differences were used, respected, and valued. Group work had direction, with participation purposely planned to sharpen group skills. The classroom atmosphere was one of diligence, cooperation, and purpose. Provision was made for oral and written expression. Creativeness was encouraged.

The work during the unit seemed to be fulfilling several functions of the educational program; those of 1. integration; 2. exploration; 3. guidance; 4. differentiation; 5. socialization; and 6. articulation of education and experiences.

The activities provided for unique social, emotional, and physical needs of the junior high age group. It emphasized intellectual growth of young adolescents with particular stress on continuing improvement in the fundamental skills. Broad, exploratory experiences were possible and special individual interests and needs were considered.

The parents, international friends, and supervising teacher learned much from, and with, the class.

Summary Statements of Appraisal and Conclusions

The brief statement of appraisal and the identification of the conclusions reached, exemplify the criteria proposed by Herrick and Estvan.[2] Evaluation is concerned with: (1) determination of the degree to which the behavior of the learners

---

[2] Helen McCracken Carpenter, editor, "Skills in Social Studies," *Twenty-Fourth Yearbook of the National Council for the Social Studies*, Chapter XII. Washington: National Council for the Social Studies, 1953, pp. 246–60.

reflects the desired educational objectives; (2) the objectives as they are related to "objectives of process to distinguish them from objectives of content" (The unit was evaluated in terms of critical thinking, organizing information, reading, listening, interpretation, and participation in group situations.); (3) development of skills, the scope and performance of the skills, and the sequence in which these operations take place; (4) a number of observations from as many vantage points as possible; (5) allowing the child to become an important observer and evaluator of his own skill behavior; and, (6) various kinds of standards which might be used to appraise skill behavior.

One of the objectives stated earlier, pertained to the development of individual skills, understandings, and attitudes that would help students to become intelligent and productive participants in society. The unit was designed in such a fashion that it appears to be in close harmony with the thoughts of Kurfman and Solomon.[3] They proposed that skills must be determined and evaluated as they relate to critical thinking, communication, development of a sense of place and time, and human relations. The conclusions arrived at, upon termination of the unit, are evidence of fulfillment of these proposed skills.

It appeared obvious, after scrutinizing the chart of Day-By-Day Activities, that pupil planning and group responsibility were integral parts of the program. The teacher assumed the role of guide and leader in helping students to organize and plan their activities. During the two hour block of time, a variety of experiences were utilized. The "competitive" spirit prevailed, but it was not allowed to promote a negative learning environment. The best principles as related to competition appear to have been employed to a high degree.

The concept of teamwork was utilized to a great extent. Opportunities were provided for cooperation and creative thinking. The committee approach allowed for effective growth in leadership. This method of working together on common problems is bound to lead to general improvement in human relations and in communication. A natural outcome of committee participation, with careful teacher guidance, is an enhanced productivity and participation. By involving foreign

students, these 7th-graders were helped in developing greater respect for other persons and they gained greater insight toward different cultures. Evaluation of the unit was continuous, involving the teacher, pupils, and ultimately, parents.

The Gestalt or organismic psychologists tell us that learning consists in the modification of behavior through experience. The individual functions as one total organism responding to constantly changing situations. The learner has purposes and when a serious gap develops between the purposes of the teacher and the pupil, negative learning may occur. Learning also involves action. If there is no provision for action, the ultimate amount of learning is negligible. Learning also involves critical thinking. This may be the most important aspect of Gestalt theory as opposed to the mental discipline concept.

Study the Chart of Day-By-Day Activities! Does this unit plan allow for experiences? Does it provide constantly changing situations? Do you think the purposes of the teacher are also purposes of the children? Is action an important part of the program? Would critical thinking be necessary? Did each individual have opportunities to perceive new experiences uniquely? Were opportunities provided for these perceptions to be shared with others in a systematic way? Do you feel that individuals were able to see themselves as being able to achieve certain goals? And, finally, were pupils better able to achieve success and enhance their own self-concept as a result of the methods and experiences employed in the "Four Foreign Friends"?

Sources of Educational Films and Materials

A. Pupil References
    1. *National Geographic Magazines* (Appropriate issues.)
    2. *Textbook*: Pounds, Norman J. G., *Beyond the Oceans*, Rand McNally, 1962.
    3. Numerous books, articles, artifacts brought in by pupils
B. General Reference Sources
    1. *Britannica Jr.*
    2. *Colliers Encyclopedia*
    3. *Compton's Pictured Encyclopedia*
    4. *Information Please Almanac Atlas and Yearbook,* Simon and Schuster
    5. *National Geographic Atlas of the World.*
    6. *Political Handbook and Atlas of the World,* Council on Foreign Relations, Harper and Row

---

[3] Helen McCracken Carpenter, editor, "Skill Development in Social Studies," *Thirty-Third Yearbook of the National Council for the Social Studies*, Chapter XIV. Washington: National Council for the Social Studies, 1963, p. 279.

7. *World Almanac and Book of Facts*, New York World Telegram and Sun.
8. *World Book*

C. People
1. Foreign-born Persons: Students, Residents
2. Travelled Persons

D. Teacher References
1. Aldrich, Julian C., Editor—*Social Studies for the Junior High School*, Curriculum Series #6; National Council for the Social Studies, NEA, Washington, D.C., 1957.
2. Anderson, Howard R., Editor, *Approaches to an Understanding of World Affairs*, National Council for the Social Studies, NEA, Washington, D.C., 1954.
3. Brown, R. A., "Improving Instruction in the Junior High School Social Studies," *Social Education* 25:1, 39–42, March, 1961.
4. What Research Says Series
   Department of Classroom Teachers, American Educational Research Association of National Education Association particularly the following titles:
      5. *Personality Adjustment of Individual Children* (Ralph H. Ojemann)
      6. *The Learning Process* (William Clark Trow)
      7. *Evaluating and Reporting Pupil Progress* (John W. M. Rothney)
      8. *Guided Study and Homework* (Ruth Strang)
      13. *Class Organization for Instruction* (J. Wayne Wrightstone)
      14. *Audio-Visual Instruction* (Paul R. Wendt)
      15. *Juvenile Delinquency* (William C. Kvaraceus)
      16. *Parent-Teacher Relationships* (Irving Wistant and Grace Langdon)
      19. *Groups Processes in Elementary and Secondary Schools* (Louis M. Smith)
      20. *Teaching the Social Studies* (Jonathon C. McLendon)
      21. *Understanding Intergroup Relations* (Jean D. Grambs)
      28. *Creativity* (E. Paul Torrence)
5. Edgar, R. W., "History, Reading and Human Relations: An Integrated Approach," *Social Education* 29:155–84, March, 1965.
6. Smith, N. C., "Reading in Subject Matter Fields; Reading in Social Studies," *Educational Leadership* 22:382–3, March, 1965.
7. Wright, Grace S., *Block-Time Classes and the Core Program*, U.S. Department of Health, Education and Welfare, Washington, D.C., 1958.
8. Zander, A., and Medare, H., "Strength of Groups and Desire for Attainable Group Aspiration," *Journal of Personality* 33: 122–39, March, 1965.

E. Educational Films (List of available titles from which several were selected for previewing and a few actually used as time or plan allowed.)

India
1. *India—Sub-Continent of Asia* (Our World of the Sixties), color, United World.
2. *Hindu Family*, black and white, Encyclopedia Britannica Films.
3. *New India*, color, EVP.
4. *India*, (Customs in the Village), Encyclopedia Britannica Films.
5. *India: Asia's New Voice*, Encyclopedia Britannica Films.

Japan
1. *Japanese Family*, International Film Foundation: Julien Bryan.
2. *Japan*, color, International Film Foundation.
3. *Japan: 80,000,000 Mouths to Feed*, color, Encyclopedia Britannica Films.
4. *Japan: The Land and the People*, Coronet Films.

Nigeria
1. *Africa in Change: West Africa*, color, Encyclopedia Britannica Films.

Southeast Asia
1. *Southeast Asia: Lands and Peoples*, Coronet Films.
2. *Siam*, (The People of Thailand), color, Walt Disney Productions.
3. *Niok* (Cambodia), color, Walt Disney Productions.
4. *Letter From Indonesia*, color, Chur.
5. *Orient, the—Peoples of Asian Lands* (Our World of the Sixties), color, United World.

Chapter 8

Social Studies in the 7th and 8th Grades

University School, University of Wyoming
Laramie, Wyoming*

The philosophy and objectives of the University School are based upon a variety of criteria. The needs of the student, community, state, nation, and the world were considered before establishing aims and objectives. The specific objectives for the social studies in the 7th and 8th grades are based upon: (1) the philosophy and objectives of the School; (2) research in psychology as related to the learning process; and (3) research in human growth and development. The unique qualities, interests, and needs of the young adolescent were emphasized in developing units for the social studies in the 7th and 8th grades. We subscribe to the concept that the only thing that remains constant, in our society, is change. Therefore, the methods employed, materials utilized, and content are continually re-evaluated and modified.

Philosophy and Objectives of University School

We believe that:

(1) The school is organized to promote and perpetuate the ideals of a democratic society. In order to fulfill its responsibilities that school should provide the environment and learning experience wherein each pupil may participate effectively in the world; (2) Educational opportunities for each child are essential for his well-being; and (3) The problem of philosophical and curricular revision is a continuous one.

Therefore, we strive to provide an environment

and learning experience which should enable youth to:

1. Understand, appreciate, and respect democratic processes so that they may:
   a. respect human dignity
   b. appreciate their privileges
   c. accept responsibilities
2. Achieve and maintain sound mental and physical health by:
   a. participating in physical activities
   b. understanding the human body
   c. practicing desirable health and safety standards
   d. developing emotional stability
3. Live the good life in the world of today through:
   a. understanding and appreciating the natural environment
   b. understanding and efficiently using scientific progress
   c. providing desirable opportunities for talented young people
   d. acting in accordance with acceptable moral and spiritual values
4. Recognize and accept sound guidance through:
   a. exploration of various human endeavors
   b. knowledge of personal strengths and weaknesses
   c. adjustment to individual limitations
5. Think logically and express themselves clearly through:
   a. efficient application of the tools of learning
   b. critical selection and effective organization of materials

---

* As reported by Mr. Harold Blankenship, Instructor, College of Education, University of Wyoming, Laramie, Wyoming.

64

c. worthwhile participation in school and community activities

6. Prepare for work, further education, or both, through:
   a. acquaintance with vocational and educational opportunities
   b. development of essential skills to secure and hold a job
   c. application of ethical practices
   d. guidance and supervision of work experiences
   e. placement and follow-up service

7. Make worthy use of their leisure time through:
   a. development of individual interests, talents, and appreciations
   b. discriminative selection and effective participation in school and community activities

8. Appreciate and live the aesthetic life by:
   a. being sensitive to the beautiful
   b. developing desirable standards of appreciation

This philosophy is implemented through the social studies, among the areas of the entire program in University School, by the following K–12 outline.

Social Studies Content
University School

Grade	Unit	Optional Units
1	Home	
	School	
	Courtesy	
	Personal Responsibility	
2	Community Helpers	
	Around the World	
3	Early Life on the Laramie Plain	Food
	Homes	Transportation
	Clothing	Christmas
	Communication	Around the World
		Origin of America's Christmas Customs
4	Wyoming's Earliest People	
	Wyoming's Desert Years	Holidays
	Return of the Buffalo	Biographies of Famous Pioneers
	Red Men of Today	
	Trappers and Traders	
	Emigrant and Treasure Trails	
	First Transcontinental Railway	

Grade	Unit	Optional Units
	Wyoming Pioneer Life	
	Rise of the Cattle Kingdom	
	Sheepmen of the Wyoming Plains	
	Wyoming Comes to Statehood	
5	Discovery and Exploration of the New World	Conservation
	Life in the Colonies	Holidays
	Making a New Nation	Thanksgiving
	The Northeastern States	Arbor Day
	Inventions Bring Changes	
	Southern States	
	Oklahoma and Texas	
	Central States	
6	The Mountainous West	Hawaii
	Moving to the Northwest	Wyoming
	The Colorful Southwest	Use and Care of Recreational Facilities
	Our Next Door Neighbor to the South (Mexico)	
	Our Sister Continent to the South (Central and South America)	Living Together in the Shrinking World
	Our Northern Neighbors	

7. Theme of World Understanding
   1. History of American democratic thought
   2. Man's search for ways to control his environment
   3. Contributions of specific nations and cultures to our ways of living today
   4. Man's attempt to live in peace and harmony
   5. The Far East
   6. Africa

Units providing exploratory experiences
   1. Propaganda
   2. Historical development of the people of specific nations
   3. Creative writing
   4. Development of various forms of writing
   5. Occupational studies
   6. World trouble spots today
   7. Literature from other countries
   8. The governments of man
   9. This planet Earth
   10. Great Americans from other countries

8. Appreciating American Culture in Its Historical

Grade	Unit	Optional Units
	Development and Present Status	
	Understanding the Political, Economic, and Social Phases of American Life	
	Relating Wyoming and the West to the National Scene	
9	First Semester: Western Civilization	
	Second Semester: Vocational Guidance and Citizenship	
10	World Geography	
	1. Weather and climate regions	
	2. Russia	
	3. British Commonwealth	
	4. Latin America	
	5. Africa	
	6. World Trade	
11	1. Colonial America	
	2. American Revolution	
	3. Critical Period and the Constitution	
	4. Federalist Period	
	5. Westward Movement and Sectionalism	
	6. Foreign Policy	
	7. Industrial v. Agrarian (Civil War)	
	8. Change of rural to urban society	
	9. U.S. as a World Power	
	10. Twentieth Century domestic problems	
12	American Problems	
	1. Juvenile Delinquency	
	2. Taxation	
	3. Conservation	
	4. Labor and Management	
	5. Education	
	6. Foreign Affairs	
	7. Minorities	
	8. Competing Philosophies of Government	

The University school is organized as one educational unit, grades kindergarten through 12. The junior high school section is a sub-division consisting of grades 7 and 8 within the six-year high school portion of the entire unit. Considerable effort is made to provide experiences appropriate for students in the 7th and 8th grades differentiated from the school activities which are typical of older students in the 9th through the 12th grades. A core plan is followed in 7th and 8th grades for social studies.

7th-Grade Core
Objectives and Subject-matter Vehicle*

I. Objectives

A. Skills

1. To further the development of all communication skills for the individual pupil including
   a. *Spelling.*
   b. *Writing.* Particular emphasis placed on sentence structure and paragraph construction.
   c. *Oral.* Including reporting, dramatics, discussion, and reading.
   d. *Reading.* Emphasis on both rate and comprehension. In addition, the pupil is introduced to and expected to achieve some skill in various kinds of reading including scientific, simple essays, poetry, and areas of reading relating to the humanities.

2. To give pupils opportunities in the practice and evaluation of those skills which are necessary in working with others in both large and small groups in a democratic setting.

3. To aid the pupil in developing study skills in all areas.

4. To introduce the pupil to skills in problem-solving techniques including the use of collected data as a basis for arriving at sound conclusions and in making valid decisions.

5. To develop basic geographical skills and understandings related to man's attempt to live in his environment on earth.

B. Appreciations

1. To enhance the appreciation of the pupil regarding the long struggle of man to achieve a democratic form of government.

2. To gain an appreciation of the contributions of other cultures to our ways of life in America.

3. To develop appreciations of the relationships present in our earth as a planet.

4. To promote appreciations of ideas of the interdependence of man in his struggle for existence.

5. To develop attitudes of appreciation toward man's attempts to conquer space.

6. To provide appreciations of knowledge as the major vehicle by which man has made advances in providing better standards of living.

7. To contribute to expanding attitudes of interest on the part of individuals through provision of exploratory experiences in related fields of knowledge.

C. Attitudes

1. To develop attitudes of the acceptance of

---

* Social Studies Curriculum Committee, *Social Studies Objectives, University School, K–12,* College of Education, University of Wyoming, 1961.

others, their strengths and weaknesses in the setting provided by the classroom and the school.

2. To strengthen attitudes of a healthy and wholesome nature of the early adolescent toward himself as a changing human being.
3. To further the development of loyalty to the larger group to which the adolescent belongs.
4. To develop attitudes of tolerance toward others, both in the school and in the larger society.
5. To promote the growth in wholesome attitudes toward home and family living and the role of the early adolescent in these settings.
6. To foster an attitude of enthusiasm for further education.
7. To further attitudes related to the necessity of self-discipline necessary for life in a democracy.

II. Subject-matter vehicle to arrive at the above objectives

A. Units of study utilizing teacher-pupil planning centered around themes of world understanding.
    1. History of American democratic thought.
    2. Man's search for ways to control his environment.
    3. Contributions of specific nations and cultures to our ways of living today.
    4. Man's attempt to live in peace and harmony.
    5. The Far East.
    6. Africa.

B. Units of study providing exploratory experiences.
    1. Propaganda.
    2. Historical development of the people of specific nations.
    3. Creative writing.
    4. Development of various forms of writing.
    5. Occupational studies.
    6. World trouble spots today.
    7. Literature from other countries.
    8. The governments of man.
    9. This planet Earth.
    10. Great Americans from other countries.

Social Studies Aims in 8th-Grade Core

I. Subject-Matter Aims
A. To develop appreciation of the American democratic heritage, its rights and responsibilities.
B. To gain knowledge of the basic facts concerning the development of our constitution, the expansion of the United States into an industrial giant, and the social and economic consequences of our national development.
C. To understand the workings of our democracy through generalization of democratic classroom procedures.

D. To become acquainted with and gain in appreciation for the qualities of leadership and ideas demonstrated by the founders and perpetuators of the American ideals.
E. To discover the roles played in American life by minority and special interest groups.
F. To develop understandings of how the state of Wyoming fits into the historical patterns of the United States.

II. Skill Aims

A. To develop the skills of individual and group problem solving.
B. To further in the reading, spelling, and study skills necessary for the individual to become a working member of society.
C. To grow in the ability to use increasing self-direction in individual and group work.
D. To gain skill in using the contributions of others to individual knowledge.

III. Attitude Aims

A. To gain a growing sense of the personal worth of each individual in the school and classroom society and in the broader community.
B. To discover the feelings of democratic living.

The Core Concept

Recognition of the personal and social needs of young adolescents at University School has led to Core classes based on teacher-pupil planning. Within the social studies and language arts, problems which concern 7th and 8th grade pupils become the means for activities and experiences which aid in achieving outcomes held to be desirable for young adolescents. Opportunity to develop basic skills is afforded through planned activities.

Hopefully, the unit that follows, exemplifies many of the features of Core. In addition to the characteristics already referred to, it allowed for teacher-pupil planning, block of time, guidance, a variety of materials, and continuous teacher-pupil evaluation. It also took into account the importance of pertinent systematic knowledge.

The faculty of the University Junior High School feels that such a Core plan is presently the best way to meet student needs. The Core concept has been utilized in the University Junior High School since 1954. At no time is it felt that Core is the final, unchangeable answer. It is only through constant evaluation and research of teaching methods, educational psychology, and educational philosophy, that teachers can remain in the mainstream of educational development. The faculty and administrators are constantly striving toward improved methods in the teaching-learning process.

Student Needs

Discovering Individual Student's Needs and Interests

Students are motivated to learn when there is an immediate reason or purpose for that learning. Hence, a student who wants to write a letter to a pen-pal might see a need for learning to write a letter correctly. A student who has an interest in guns might become interested in the study of weaponry and how the invention of gunpowder influenced the stream of history. Needs and interests of the students can be used by the teacher to motivate learning. First, however, the teacher must discover the needs and interests of the students. Standardized tests, personality inventories, projective techniques are some of the ways that interests of students can be discovered. A student inventory sheet can be devised by the teacher for the students to complete. Such questions as: "What do you do in the afternoon after school?", "What hobbies do you have?", "What are your favorite games?" can help the teacher a great deal in identifying students' interests outside the classroom. This type of questionnaire can reveal student need. For example, the student who has no outside interests is certainly exhibiting an unfilled need. One of the characteristics of the young adolescent is his need to participate in activities outside the home and the classroom. The promotion of leisure time activities is thought by some to be outside the realm of the public school; but is it? Each individual, especially the young adolescent, should be encouraged to develop an interest in a hobby or other leisure-time activity.

Needs are further expressed by the student in the classroom by his actions. It is up to the skillful teacher to interpret these actions in terms of needs and to guide the student in meaningful classroom experiences. In this way, the student who has a need for attention can be easily recognized. The quiet, shy child can be exhibiting a need for security and self-confidence. The boastful, bullying child can be looking for attention. The need for success is a universal need of all people. Certainly, this is true of the young adolescent.

The Program

Introduction to the Core Program at University Junior High School

The University Junior High School Core class is not organized along traditional lines. Even though Social Studies and Language Arts compose the core of the program, the students and the teachers are not limited to a textbook curriculum. Factual information is not ignored, but it is not an end in itself. Facts are acquired strictly for their utilitarian value.

Processes of the Core Program

As has been previously indicated, the Core program at University School is not bound to a textbook or curriculum guide though both are available as resource materials.

The emphasis is placed upon group problem-solving and pupil-teacher planning. Units are tentatively outlined. These areas of interests are often changed and modified; however, the initial planning gives a working, meaningful outline. To illustrate, the proposed unit topics for the 7th and 8th grade Core classes in September of 1965, are listed. Topics were of interest and concern to the students. The list will be evaluated and modified because the time element may prevent completion.

Proposed Unit Topics for 7th-Grade Core 1965–1966

1. State and Local Government
2. American Indians
3. Communism and Democracy
4. The Movement West
5. Presidents of the United States
6. Continents of the World

Proposed Unit Topics for 8th-Grade Core 1965–1966

1. Teenagers: Yesterday, Today, and Tomorrow
2. Transportation and Communication
3. Countries of the World
4. History of Weapons
5. Religions and Man

As an individual unit progresses, detailed expansion of the topics are chosen for large scale units; sub-topics are selected for committee work. Individual assignments are made within the committee structure. A weekly work plan is made out each Monday. A suggested outline which evolved from the 8th-grade unit on Teenagers follows to illustrate specific plans for a unit.

Teenagers—Yesterday, Today, and Tomorrow 8th-Grade Core Unit

Outline

I. Music and Food
  A. Music of Yesterday
    1. Dances
    2. Singers and groups
    3. Idols

B. Music of Today
 1. Dances
 2. Singers and groups
 3. What goes into it all
 4. Idols
C. Music of Tomorrow
 1. Changing styles
 2. Non-music
 3. Where do we go from here?
D. Eating Habits Yesterday
 1. Dinners
 2. Lunches
 3. Snacks
 4. Breakfast
E. Eating Habits of Today
 1. Dinners
 2. Lunches
 3. Snacks
 4. Breakfast
II. Clothes, Hairstyles and Accessories (Boys and Girls)
A. Hairstyles
 1. Yesterday
 2. Today
 3. Tomorrow
B. Accessories
 1. Yesterday
 2. Today
 3. Tomorrow
C. Make-up (Girls only)
 1. Yesterday
 2. Today
 3. Tomorrow
D. Clothes
 1. Formal
 2. Informal
 3. Sportswear
 4. Nightwear
III. Getting Along
A. Parents
B. Teachers
C. Other teenagers
D. Ourselves
E. Some problems
IV. Modes of Transportation and Communication
A. Automobiles
B. Motorcycles
C. Hot Rods
D. Radio
E. Television
F. Telephone
V. Teenagers of Foreign Lands
A. Syria
B. Greece
C. Egypt
D. Norway
VI. Hobbies
A. Photography
B. Rockets
C. Trains and Cars
D. Stamps and Coins
E. Models
VII. Juvenile Delinquency
A. Gangs
B. Narcotics
C. Vandalism
D. Crime and Punishment
VIII. Summary and Evaluation

The problem-solving approach to learning is utilized. Each student has a topic or problem that must be researched and reported to the class. This activity fits into the framework of the small committee topic which in turn relates to the main unit. The teachers and students plan the evolving unit and the students are encouraged to evaluate their work continually.

In Core, group work toward common goals permits actual experiences in learning to work cooperatively. Individual reports, based on research, provide opportunities for written and oral presentations. In the process certain subject areas are vehicles, or tools:

Creative Writing
English Grammar
Reading (remedial and/or enrichment)
Spelling
Current Events

While the students are working on a unit of study, they will be involved in activities such as:

Research (in the classroom and library)
Writing reports
Group work (large and small groups)
Oral reporting
Note taking
Planning
Scheduling

In addition to the tangible activities listed above, the students will also be in the process of:

Self-evaluation
Cooperation
Sharing
Participation
Responsibility (to the individual and to the group)
Democracy
Critical thinking

One of the results of the aforementioned activities was the school newspaper, "Junior Hi-Lites." The paper was suggested by the students and is published periodically (usually once each month) by the Core classes. The paper contains articles written by the students for the students. Various types of articles are included. The publication generally centers around the Units being studied within Core class and enriches the classroom program.

Evaluation of the Core Program

Continual evaluation on the part of teachers and students is essential in the Core program. It is when the student reaches an objective self-appraisal that real values become evident. This self-evaluation gives a clear view of what has been done and the personal growth that has taken place. Within the evaluation procedure, the student can understand himself better, grow in personal-social relationships, and better understand his contemporaries. It is hoped that by thinking through these relationships, respect for the other person will become a way of life.

Students are aided in evaluating their progress in individual skills by keeping folders of their work and checking periodically to see what progress and improvement has been made.

A Unit in Action

Introduction

Last year with the approach of Pan-American Day, interest grew in both the 7th and the 8th-grade Core classes from comments by students based on their knowledge or curiosity regarding Latin American peoples. From this discussion by pupils and teacher came the proposal that a project for Pan-American Day be undertaken. This suggestion was met with approval in both classes. A joint meeting of the 7th and the 8th-grade class officers was called. Invitations were sent to the school principal, school librarian, parents, and members of the two classes involved who were interested and wished to attend. The purpose of the meeting was to decide on general areas of study, some broad general objectives, and how the rather broad topic of Latin America might best be approached.

Planning the Unit

The planning-session meeting was well attended. In fact it was so well attended that it was decided to divide the participants into three groups; each group had the responsibility of discussing a problem. Group One outlined "General Areas of Study;" Group Two, "General Objectives;" and Group Three devised a "Plan of Action."

Each group or committee (four to five members) was instructed to select a chairman and a recorder and to be prepared to report to the group in twenty minutes. The groups reported as follows:

Group I: General Areas of Study
   A. Countries or Regions
   B. Natural Resources
   C. Interdependence with each other and the United States
Group II: General Objectives (These are accomplished by means of a variety of methods and teaching-learning materials)

Self Evaluation Check List
Junior High Core

	O*	S*	I*	N*
Reading and Literature				
Reads with understanding				
Reads at a satisfactory rate				
Uses appropriate skills				
Reads well orally				
Reads and enjoys good books				
Effort				
Language (speaking, writing, listening)				
Expresses ideas clearly in discussion				
Evidence knowledge of use of grammar				
Shows growth in use of new words				
Writes a good sentence, paragraph				
Spelling progress				
Writes neatly and legibly				
Effort				
Social Studies				
Interprets maps, charts, graphs				
Takes part in group discussion				
Shows knowledge of current events				
Analyzes materials				
Makes good use of reference materials				
Uses facts in the solution of problems				
Effort				
Social and Emotional Development				
Is courteous and cooperative				
Respects rights of others				
Gets along well with others				
Respects authority				
Shows growth in self control				
Accepts responsibility				
Work Habits and Attitudes				
Takes pride in work				
Uses school time wisely				
Follows directions carefully				
Completes work on time				
Thinks for himself				
Is attentive in class				
Is developing good study skills				
Goes beyond assigned work				

* O = Outstanding
  S = Satisfactory
  I = Improving
  N = Not Improving

A. Conceptual learnings about people and cultures of other countries
B. Relationships of climatic conditions to economic development
C. Understanding of the organization of American States
D. Learnings about the Aztecs, Incas, and Mayas
E. Understanding of the influence of the early Spanish explorers on present day Latin America (Other topics such as the Panama Canal, Monroe Doctrine, and Religion were mentioned. However, it was decided that the interests of the students and time would be the final arbitrators for General Objectives.)

Group III: Plan of Action
A. Committee and Individual Reports
B. Exhibits
C. Festival
(Since Pan-American Day was coming in less than two weeks, Group 3 felt that concerted effort should be directed toward terminating the unit with a celebration for that day.)

(It should be noted here that the 7th and 8th grades do not usually work together on the same unit. They have Core at different times of the day, so this unit was unique in that both classes would be correlating their work even though they would not be meeting together during the scheduled school day.)

Presentation of Unit

The next day each class was given the report and suggestions from the Planning Committee. That afternoon after school, a Steering Committee, composed of four members of each class, met with the teachers to revise the Unit Plan. In this final revision, the suggestions of the students were used to augment the suggestions of the Planning Committee.

The Revised Unit Plan was quite similar to the plan submitted by the Planning Committee. The main difference was that items B and C of the General Areas of Study would become two additional General Objectives. This means that the Areas of Study would be Countries of Central and South America. The General Objectives, the students agreed, were rather long and involved for only seven days of study. However, they would be explored as adequately as time and resource material would permit. The Plan of Action remained intact. Reports on the different countries would be prepared, exhibits of artifacts and pictures of the various countries would be set up in the classroom, and on Pan-American Day the entire school day would be devoted to listening to reports, viewing films, and participation in the luncheon which was planned to provide typical Latin American dishes. In addition, the classroom would be decorated with crepe paper and balloons to further the festive atmosphere.

Committees were organized and the students were permitted to select the committee or committees (limit of two) on which they wanted to work. The committees were the following:

1. *Coordinating Committee.* To act as liaison between the two classes, check on the progress of each committee, and schedule the activities for Pan-American Day.

2. *Decorating Committee.* To string crepe paper, hang balloons, and arrange for tables for the luncheon.

3. *Exhibit Committee.* Although all students were asked to bring Latin-American artifacts and anything they could beg or borrow that came from Latin America, this Committee's job was to arrange these for display in the classroom.

4. *Reporting Committee.* To do research and write reports on the various countries.

5. *Film Committee.* To review and select films for viewing.

6. *Bulletin Board Committee.* To find, select, and display pictures the Reporting Committee needed to illustrate reports.

7. *Luncheon Committee.* To select recipes typical of Latin America and obtain volunteers (mothers) to prepare the food.

8. *Invitations Committee.* To write and send invitations for the Pan-American Day Festival to local dignitaries. Included on the list, among others, were the University President, the editor of the local newspaper, the faculty and administrators of the University School and College of Education and past student teachers of the Junior High Core classes.

9. *Miscellaneous Committee.* To take care of unexpected details that required committee action.

It should be emphasized that although this was a joint undertaking of the 7th (31 members) and the 8th (32 members) grades they did not have their Core class at the same time of the day. Therefore, it was necessary for the committees to meet after school to plan what the members of each grade would do during the time their respective Core classes met. The members of each committee were students from both grades, so these after-school committee meetings were necessary for each committee member to know what he was supposed to do and what had been done.

During the class work on the units, the students in both classes were also involved in other activities related to the units. All Core students were required to have a reading book at all times, and usually spent thirty minutes of each Core class reading. The books were selected by the students from the school library, and most students read a book each week. The students were also involved in giving book reports, individual interest reports, spelling, and any other activities related to the needs and/or interests of the students.

The unit on Latin America is much too important to limit the students to acquiring a few facts about some of the countries south of the border. There is much more involved. Planning, researching, discussing, reading, writing, thinking, working, telling, listening, and organizing are samples of what is involved in a core unit; and so the work continues. Committee meetings, progress reports, gathering materials, collecting data, revising reports, rewriting, and comparing notes are just part of the day's work.

The day before the Festival, the final progress reports were presented orally by the committee chairman. The work was complete. Everything was ready. The goal had been reached.

Evaluation

The final phase of a core unit is evaluation. This is done for two reasons: (1) to see what has been done; and (2) to see what each member of the class has accomplished by doing these things. Time was set aside the day after the Festival for evaluation. The classes were divided into small buzz groups, and each group was to make a list of all the things that had been done. At the side of each item listed, the students were to indicate their personal accomplishments. For example:

Activity	*Accomplishments*
Decorating the Room	Planning, working together, sharing ideas, choosing "go-together" colors
Writing Invitations	Learning how to write invitations, sentence structure, creativity
Oral Reports	Doing research, writing, planning, paragraphing, speaking before a group
Group Work	Sharing ideas, listening, planning, working together, cooperating, discussing, compromising, leading, following
Research Projects	Learning how to use reference materials, learning to use the library, working independently, taking notes, how to summarize what has been read
Writing Reports	Learning how to outline, sentence structure, penmanship, following directions, using dictionary

The completed list was three typewritten pages, and some of the students felt it was not complete. This feeling resulted in ideas for further research. Two students felt that they would like to know more about the Alliance for Progress. Their joint report, two days later, was most enlightening. Another student became interested in Simon Bolivar. The pupil was referred to the biography section of the school library. Two others in the group became pen-pals with two students residing in Mexico City. Two weeks later "Latin America" was still being discussed even though the students were involved in a rather intensive study of Spain to research the origin of Latin Americans.

Conclusion

Various reasons could be given for having a Core program, but they all evolve from one source. It is felt that Core is an effective way to teach young adolescents. Volumes have been written about Core; most writers, whether they are for or against Core, agree that something "special" is required for the young adolescent. They are not in agreement about what is needed, but they do feel that more than the "traditional approach" to subject matter is desirable for this age group.

The 7th- and 8th-graders fit into the Social Studies pattern of the total school's curriculum as it serves as a bridge, linking together the elementary and high school programs. The vehicle for building this bridge is the Language Arts—Social Studies program.

Section III

Meeting the Challenge of Social Studies Instruction
In the Junior High School

Chapter 9

Meeting the Challenge of Social Studies Instruction In the Junior High School

Eugene Cottle
Professor of Social Studies Education
University of Wyoming
Laramie, Wyoming

The young adolescent in today's social environment is sensitive to many powerful influences which must be recognized as factors in his development. As explained in Chapter 1 by Gruhn, the young adolescent responds in many ways which reveal early social maturing. Because the school is the one institution designated by society to bring youth into effective membership in the society, we find the junior high school adjusting its program to the needs of the young adolescent who has encountered new and different problems arising from the many cultural innovations of our day and from his own developmental growth. As Johnson explains in Chapter 2, the junior high school has turned to the social studies to a considerable extent for its principal means of bringing desirable learning experiences to the maturing individual who at this age level is seeking personal-social adjustment and the many skills he needs in living. Johnson has pointed out that it becomes the responsibility of the junior high school to guide individuals into satisfactory participation in their culture.

Perhaps the most effective preparation for membership in the adult society is the pursuit of excellence in the areas of general education which will develop the individual's abilities to meet the problems yet unknown and for which no specific preparation can be made. A committee of the National Council for the Social Studies has expressed the purpose of education in the social studies as the development of desirable socio-civic and personal behavior.[1] This necessitates that the school consider the child both in the present and as a developing citizen. Such guidance is possible, however, only if the junior high school program brings general education to the learners who are recognized in their individuality, as pointed out by Lounsbury in Chapter 3.

Section II presents the programs of some schools expressing varying philosophies ranging from a subject-centered approach, through teacher-pupil planning and core organization to the least traditional type, the ungraded school.

Section III summarizes some of the practices of these schools and proposes some suggestions for the improvement of social studies teaching in grades 7, 8, and 9. These suggestions are discussed under the following questions:

How may individual pupil needs be discovered and used?

How shall the program of learning be defined and organized?

How may Teacher-Community-School relations contribute to improved social studies instruction?

How May Individual Pupil Needs Be Discovered and Used?

The kind of philosophy which guides a school system will determine the degrees of concern which

---

[1] Statement prepared for the National Council for the Social Studies, "The Role of the Social Studies," *Social Education*, 26:315, October, 1962.

that system has for determining pupil competencies and for meeting immediate pupil needs. The problem of balance in the curriculum[2] is ever present and requires that a decision be made on the question of whether emphasis shall be on the child's present needs or upon the mastery of subject matter as the key to the adult requirements for living.

Presented in specific or in general terms, the objectives of the five school programs vary in the proportion of concern for pupil needs, the recognition of desirable pupil competence, and those needs which reflect the adult society. If the implications of Johnson's analysis are followed, more attention must be given to ways of adapting young adolescents' needs, interests, and abilities to the current society.

Determine Essential Competencies for Young Adolescents

Statements of objectives appearing in the programs of the five schools described in Section II imply the competencies needed by young adolescents. A committee in California[3] has listed the imperative needs of junior high school youth. Whether the statements of particular schools are analyzed, or an arbitrary, generalized list of needs is examined, it appears that the determination of competencies has often been done through a very traditional interpretation of the educational experience at the junior high school level. If competency to live in today's world is a need of junior high youth, as it is implied in the objectives listed by the several schools in Section II, then it appears that today's junior high school curriculum must question very seriously a point of view which expresses the function of the junior high school of a quarter of a century ago.

The industrial revolution of the last half of the 20th Century has created emphatic and radically different tasks for education, tasks whose emphasis must begin with the junior high school. These tasks express the competencies needed by junior high pupils, and they may be summarized as the intellectual abilities required of all citizens. As cited

by Johnson in Section I, the competencies of the citizen in an advanced society are largely of an intellectual nature: the acquisition of basic knowledge and significant ideas, of skills and habits of inquiry and thought, and the abilities needed to understand human behavior as well as to function effectively in a society where extensive leisure, automated production, and planning have revised the human perspective.

The Commission on Secondary Curriculum of the Association for Supervision and Curriculum Development describes young adolescents as individuals who have:

1. A sense of positive self-worth and an enhanced understanding of others
2. A genuine interest and strengthened competence in several areas of learning, and acquaintance with the world of work
3. Mastery of basic skills of inquiry and study so that independent work may be pursued more adequately
4. An increased capacity to discipline themselves to work, to study and play constructively and with satisfaction to themselves and others
5. A moral and ethical sense which values the goals and processes of a free society[4]

The objectives of the Setauket program in social studies express substantial concern for the intellectual development demanded of a citizen in the stated aims:

1. To stimulate a curiosity for and an understanding of the study of man and his institutions.
2. To develop an understanding of the individual's place in society.
3. To encourage active participation and leadership in our society.

A plan of continuous evaluation of pupils arranged in a pattern of daily and weekly conferences between teachers and pupils and among teachers serves to implement the objectives effectively for the individual pupil.

In the Wichita Public Schools[5] the needs of the adult society are implied as aims of the planned educational experiences of youth in intellectual, civic, cultural, and vocational development.

---

[2] Halversen, Paul M., Ch., *Balance in the Curriculum*, 1961 Yearbook. Washington, D.C.: Association for Supervision and Curriculum Development, National Education Association, 1961, pp. 10–16.

[3] Herriott, M. E., Sands, Elizabeth, and Stauffacher, Harvey W., "History and Objectives of Junior High Education in California," *Bulletin of the National Association of Secondary School Principals*, 31:14–19, December, 1951.

[4] Association for Supervision and Curriculum Development, *The Junior High School We Need*. Washington, D.C.: Report from ASCD Commission on Secondary Education, NEA, 1961, prepared by Jean D. Grambs, Clarence G. Noyce, Franklin Patterson, and John Robertson, p. 3.

[5] Wichita Public School System, *Personnel Policies for the Classroom Teacher*. Wichita, Kansas: September 16, 1963.

Among the aims of University School at Southern Illinois University are several which recognize competencies needed by the individual in his growth toward adulthood and in his social responsibilities of citizenship:

8. To develop in each individual the desire and ability to understand the rights and duties of the citizen of a democratic society and to perform his obligations as a member of the community, of the state, of the nation, and of the world.
9. To develop in each individual the desire to respect other persons regardless of age, creed, or race.
10. To develop in each individual proper attitudes concerning the significance of the family for the individual and society, and an understanding of the conditions conducive to successful family life.
11. To develop in each individual skills, understanding, and attitudes that will make him an intelligent and productive participant in economic life.

The concern for achieving effective social living by pupils in the McLoughlin Junior High School program of social studies[6] is revealed in the following selected objectives:

2. To provide experiences and build skills which will aid in the development of responsible citizenship in a democracy.
5. To create an awareness that man must adapt to changing conditions.
7. To develop the ability to solve effectively social problems through intelligent use of the scientific method.
13. To understand the problems which arise because of population growth, mobility of people, technological advancements, business expansion, and government functions.

Certainly of equal significance to the demands of the adult world are the needs of the young adolescent in his present stage of development. His concern for personal interests, some of which are potentially serious emotional and social problems, requires attention through guidance to afford a stable and poised outlook and to develop the ability to relate constructively with his environment. As Johnson implies in Section I, there are problems of adolescence with which the social studies in junior high school cannot become involved. Problems of general social interaction in the classroom afford ample opportunity for the development of essential social skills.

Skills relating to knowledge must be evaluated and developed. The abilities which enable the young adolescent to analyze data, to generalize findings, and to communicate his ideas are skills needed for the efficient understanding of knowledge.

Discover Aptitudes, Interests, and Achievements of Individual Pupils

Becoming acquainted with individual pupils is essential for the teacher if all these competencies are to be developed. Teacher observation of pupils in situations where specific skills must be applied will indicate the level of skills of each pupil. Individual conferences, questionnaires, and opinion-polls can be revealing as to pupils' personal-social attitudes, anxieties, or desires. The questionnaire can give a clue to pupil values concerning a variety of relationships. It is important to know the adolescent's idea regarding participation in activities with his peers, since much of the social learning in junior high school depends upon group relationships. Does he like to participate? Does he feel left out of some group? Does he value the group relationship? When pupils are asked to list the kinds of activities in which they are engaged, a pattern of relationships such as leadership, creativeness, initiative, or other significant social qualities may be apparent. Sociometry can assist the teacher in discovering social characteristics of individuals by using classroom procedures for the tabulating of isolates, rejected pupils, leaders, and strong group ties.

The cumulative files of pupils should also be noted as the obvious source for several kinds of information about pupils, such as data from former teachers, from parents, and from health and attendance records.

The theory of developmental tasks is familiar to those who have witnessed the movement which recognizes the importance of the whole child in the learning situation. Havighurst[7] emphasizes the forces which drive and control the individual and which challenge him to satisfactory achievement. The *Mooney Problems Checklist* can be of great assistance in discovering personal-social concerns of young adolescents.[8] To provide for the individual in his specific needs despite the circumstances

---

[6] Vancouver Public Schools, *Program of Social Studies.*

[7] Havighurst, Robert J., *Developmental Tasks and Education.* New York: Longmans, Green and Co., 1952.
[8] Mooney, Ross L., *Mooney Problems Checklist, Form J.* Columbus, Ohio: Bureau of Educational Research, Ohio State University, 1950.

which necessitate the mass approach, various curricular techniques are being explored. Valuable
assistance to the teacher is available in the 1964
Yearbook of ASCD, *Individualizing Instruction*.
When pupils know that they are accepted and
valued as individuals, they can relate effectively,
their problems can be discussed objectively, and
they are not frustrated by fear of ridicule or mis-
understanding. Teacher-pupil interaction, while
essential to provide an open situation for learning,
cannot provide the final experience for the child's
development, which must be an inner experience.
Self-discovery[9] must be encouraged in the teaching-learning situation.

Examination of the programs described in Section II reveals various procedures employed in
these schools to discover aptitudes and interests
of pupils and to involve pupils in planning and
evaluating their experiences. At the University
School of Southern Illinois University and in the
core classes at the University of Wyoming University School, group and individual conferences
have been employed. Questionnaires have been
used to discover areas of interest, and from these
responses a consensus has evolved to set the stage
for a problem study. Much motivation of pupils
has resulted from the inclusion of pupil questions
and through the use of evaluative techniques, including self-evaluation as noted in the program of
University School at Southern Illinois University.

Not all individual traits are of significance to
the school, but certainly those which effect behavioral learning and intellectual growth must be
considered. At Setauket Junior High School it is
evident that much attention has been given to the
discovery and development of knowledge skills,
of maturity of judgment, of personal-social interest, and of general aptitude. This program creates
strong motivation for each child and attempts to
provide for the individual in considerable detail
through individual conferences and through staff
evaluation of each pupil's progress.

Involve Pupils in Planning and Evaluating Learning Experiences

The junior high school must provide opportunity
for exploration by the young adolescent. Through
the quest for understanding of his environment
the young adolescent comes to an understanding
of himself. As John Dewey explained, education
is the reorganization of experience to produce

meaning and thus to enlarge the ability to guide
one's further course of action.[10] The accumu-
lated information which each pupil has in his
experience background must be the source of
ideas to enable him to explore his present environment. It is the teacher's task to open vistas
of a further range of experience in the pupil's
thinking as the young adolescent is brought into
an exploratory experience involving his cultural
environment. The response that the learner makes
to presented material reveals to the teacher significant information about that pupil as an individual
personality in process of developing. It reveals that
pupil's perceptive ability, his sensitivity to social
relationships, and his power of reflective thinking.
As the learner reacts with questions, with expressions of associated experience, with desire to learn
more about the current issue, the teacher is enabling the learner to involve himself in the planning
of the learning experience. In such involvement
there should be freedom for the pupil to express
attitudes. It is more difficult, as Taba[11] has indicated, to carry on evaluation of thinking which
involves value judgments, but this type of teacher-
pupil planning and discussion is essential in the
exploratory effort of the junior high school. It is
through such open discussion that democracy is
implemented, and pupils develop personal worth
as citizens. The freedom which is felt by a pupil
in sharing his ideas, in questioning, and in pro-
posing new applications of previously held concepts affects his concept of himself,[12] especially in
his sense of independence, a phase of development
very important for the young adolescent.

Plan Significant Learning Experiences of Recognized Personal-Social-Civic Value for Individual Pupils

A basic factor in planning significant learning
experiences for young adolescents is the element
of personal involvement in the activity. When the
pupil helps to design the activity, he is expressing
his own need and purpose. Also involved in the
act of learning should be that developmental
quality that gives an enduring meaning to an
experience as it builds the possibility of future
association in a later learning experience. Such

---

[9] Association for Supervision and Curriculum Development, *Individualizing Instruction*, 1964 Yearbook. Washington, D.C.: ASCD, NEA, 1964, p. 92.

[10] Dewey, John, *Democracy and Education*. New York:
Macmillan, 1916, pp. 89–90.

[11] Association for Supervision and Curriculum Development, *New Insights and the Curriculum*. Washington,
D.C.: ASCD, NEA, 1963, p. 239.

[12] Shaftel, Fannie R., "Toward More Autonomy for
Learners," *New Insights and the Curriculum*. Washington, D.C.: ASCD Yearbook, 1963, pp. 122–123.

learning experience may best be described in terms of problem-solving, an approach widely recognized although not practiced to a proportionate degree.

As indicated in the program of University School, University of Wyoming, and in the University School at Southern Illinois University, the problems approach is well exemplified. Caution must be observed in following the problems approach as Casey and Muessig[13] suggest. The problem should be of worthwhile significance, educationally justifiable, appropriate to the age level, and not limited in scope. For a truly behavioral influence, problem-solving should afford the pupil an open exploration. Teaching by definition has no place in the true problem-solving technique. Probably one of the greatest benefits to be achieved for the learner in problem-solving is the development of knowledge skills. To search out information and to evaluate data in terms of satisfactory solutions or broadened understanding of problems are valuable experiences. To use the information in a further range of experience rather than merely answering a question influences the behavioral aspects of learning.[14] The open discussion allowing the child to express his thought in a situation where he realizes his values are being recognized establishes habits of critical analysis of his environment in a poised and unemotional atmosphere.

How Shall the Program of Learning Be Defined and Organized?

The decade of the 1960's has been marked by an anxiety regarding the effectiveness of the school and a sense of urgency that the educational program be shaped quickly. This attitude, expressed by educators, the pseudoeducators, and laymen, has been increasingly evident since World War II as noted by Samford and Cottle writing in the post-war period.[15] Questions regarding the content of the social studies curriculum were raised during the war years in much the same vein as questions are being asked today. Shall the curriculum emphasize facts, or shall it call for the personal-social involvement of pupils in broad understandings and

concepts of the principles of American life?[16] Leadership by the National Council for the Social Studies in curriculum evaluation anticipated the time of social adjustment following World War II in the booklet, *The Social Studies Look Beyond the War*[17] appearing in November, 1944, which stated that a curriculum would be needed that did not overlook the problems and tensions of young people because of a disproportionate emphasis upon formal learning.

This implied dichotomy is cited more recently by Dorothy Fraser in the report of curriculum study conducted by the National Education Association in relation to Project on Instruction[18] where two conditions of the social studies are recognized, namely, that seven disciplines (anthropology, economics, geography, history, political science, social psychology, and sociology) contribute to the curriculum content and that the problems of society deriving from human relations and the institutions of society form a matrix within which the social studies program must be designed.

Writing in 1964, John Goodlad called attention to the growing interest in the social science disciplines,[19] as such, in the curriculum with attention to the concepts and methods of the discrete academic areas. A somewhat parallel development within this time of curricular investigation was the attention given to the values of the behavioral sciences as these are seen to be interwoven in the broad understandings which should contribute to the pupil's learning.[20] It appears that the issue confronting the curriculum planner is the problem of making the subject matter of the social sciences significant to the pupil within the present social scene. The most comprehensive effort toward the solution of this problem has been made in Project Social Studies[21] under the direction of the United States Office of Education. Beginning in 1963, research centers for the social studies were established at several institutions of higher learning. Planning and investigating in the application of

---

13 Gross, Richard E., R. H. Muessig, and G. L. Fersh, eds., *The Problems Approach and the Social Studies*, Curriculum Series No. 9. Washington, D.C.: National Council for the Social Studies, NEA, 1960, pp. 53–54.

14 Cottle, Eugene, "The Core Class Encourages Democratic Skills," *Wyoming Education News*, 23:9–10, 22, November, 1956.

15 Samford, Clarence D., and Cottle, Eugene, *Social Studies in the Secondary School*. New York: McGraw-Hill Book Co., Inc., 1952, pp. 320–341.

16 *Ibid.*, p. 323.

17 *Ibid.*, p. 327.

18 Fraser, Dorothy M., *Current Curriculum Studies in Academic Subjects*. Washington, D.C.: National Education Association, 1962, p. 73.

19 Goodlad, John I., *School Curriculum Reform in the United States*. New York: The Fund for the Advancement of Education, 1964, p. 42.

20 Michaelis, John U., "Social Studies," *Using Current Curriculum Developments*. Washington, D.C.: The Association for Supervision and Curriculum Development, 1963, p. 73.

21 Project Social Studies, Cooperative Research Program, Office of Education, U.S. Department of Health, Education and Welfare, Washington, D.C.

social science concepts to the social studies curriculum were to proceed for five years, hopefully to produce curricular designs and materials for a new social studies curriculum. Each of the participating institutions[22] has set up a plan of its own with no apparent attempt to consider the contemporary efforts of other institutions. From this wide range of experimental proposals perhaps the public schools may draw ideas and suggestions to establish a social studies curriculum for their needs. This assumption which must be drawn must recognize some inherent weaknesses. Those projects which consider the junior high school, directly or indirectly, are being carried on at the University of Illinois, Northwestern University, the University of Georgia, the University of Minnesota, and the Carnegie Institute of Technology.

With the greater attention to subject matter of the social science disciplines being emphasized in the curriculum, it is worthy of note that economics has received possibly greater recognition among the traditional members of this group while an interest in anthropology has accorded that social science a place which it has not hitherto known in the social studies curriculum. New approaches to the study of economics at the 9th-grade level have been explored in the Curriculum Development Center at Carnegie Institute of Technology.[23] Investigations in the contributions to the social studies curriculum from anthropology have been conducted at the University of Georgia[24] and in the Anthropology Curriculum Study Project in Chicago, where teaching materials have been prepared for public school use.[25] The units prepared by the project relate to world history and are intended to aid pupils in understanding their own culture. Opportunity to apply the scientific method in anthropology is made possible. The discovery method encourages pupils to decide for themselves certain cultural principles based upon the available evidence.

In summary, as we consider the effort to revise and improve the social studies curriculum, it becomes evident that the classroom teacher must be a deciding factor in whatever innovation or revision is made. Many formal investigations of the curriculum may be carried on by organized teams which conduct experimental studies and prepare materials based upon the experiments. Such efforts and their resulting materials will not of themselves bring changes in the social studies curriculum. The teacher's understanding of ideas which have appeared through the vast curriculum study as desirable goals in place of former concepts will be determined by the experience of the teacher. It is furthermore being recognized more fully today that a variety of limitations and restrictions influence the teacher in the classroom.[26]

Elsewhere in this volume it has been pointed out that the philosophy of a school is the controlling factor in curriculum planning. For the social studies this presents a serious over-all influence. With the return to an emphasis upon the social science disciplines in the curriculum and an incipient trend of high school subjects moving into the junior high school years, the growing philosophy of education seems to indicate a diminishing concern for the needs of young adolescents. The uncertainty of what the program of social studies should be is probably augmented by the lack of teachers who are prepared especially for the junior high school.

Among the programs presented in Section II, a K–12 sequence of the social studies curriculum is found in the McLoughlin Junior High School, Southern Illinois University School, and in Robinson Junior High School to determine what shall be taught and how that content shall be most effectively organized. The problem of selection and organization of material is ever present. Recent curriculum studies indicate serious attention being given to sequential development of basic concepts.[27] Some comments are offered concerning these programs and suggestions for the improvement of the junior high school social studies curriculum are presented in this section.

Establish Goals of Knowledge, Attitudes, and Skills Desirable for Young Adolescents

Curriculum revision has experienced a great impetus in recent years as teachers are faced with the problem of choices from among the great increase in knowledge and materials. A trend to define basic concepts has been noted in programs

[22] See *Social Education*, 29(April, 1965).

[23] Fenton, Edwin, *Teaching the New Social Studies in Secondary Schools*. New York: Holt, Rinehart, and Winston, Inc., 1966, pp. 348–365.

[24] Rice, Marion J., and Bailey, Wilfred C., "A Sequential Curriculum in Anthropology for Grades 1–7," *Social Education*, 29: 211–212, April, 1965.

[25] Anthropology Curriculum Study Project, 5632 Kimbark Avenue, Chicago, Illinois 60637.

[26] Lindsey, Margaret, "Decision-Making and the Teacher," *Curriculum Crossroads*. Columbia University, New York: Teachers College Press, Teachers College, 1962, pp. 27–40.

[27] Fraser, Dorothy M., "Status and Expectations of Current Research and Development Projects," *Social Education*, 29:421–434, November, 1965.

to revise social studies.[28] To discover basic concepts should be a joint enterprise of teachers and pupils working together. Such experience by young adolescents can also be a dynamic influence in building habits of analyzing information, of "learning how to learn." This is an application of problem-solving in a very meaningful way for the young adolescent.

To seek out basic concepts implies the acquisition of desirable knowledge through problem-solving. This meaningful experience of discovering the structure of a discipline can, as Bruner states,[29] reveal principles which, because they are understood by the learner, will reduce forgetting which follows memorization.

Evidence shows that in many school systems the structure of knowledge has been of great concern to those who have designed the program. In social studies there has been an attempt to set up an orderly progression of subject matter leading from simple to more complex relationships. This theory of the widening horizons seems to have had an extensive acceptance.[30] It is stated as the plan of curriculum design in the program of Southern Illinois University School and is implied in the programs at Vancouver and Wichita. Despite this acceptance in many school systems, the experience and social-emotional development of children at the present time offers a challenge of denial to the validity of the theory.[31] Ruth Ellsworth has pointed out that the entire world comes to a child's attention very early because of rapid communication.[32]

As teachers and pupils plan together the procedures to be followed in examining the situations which develop in the day-to-day process of the classroom, the many concepts which become significant to the learner can be a pattern of relationships for each individual as he interprets and discovers meaning for himself. It seems that the learning experience, then, becomes the curriculum, and the learning should have order, pattern, and continuity for the individual. This does not reduce the importance of subject matter but rather causes it to become more meaningful to the learner. To improve the goals of knowledge, attitudes, and skills needed for young adolescents calls for the planning of objectives, not in terms of subject matter, but as living experiences symbolized by concepts. The analysis and application of subject matter to create concepts afford learning to the individual. Such experience becomes a point of departure for subsequent experiences, thus establishing a continuity of learning.

The approach to curriculum organization which recognizes the K–12 plan seems to afford the most appropriate plan for building a continuity of learning. The concepts proposed in the *Guide to Content in the Social Studies* (recently revised under the title *Social Studies in Transition: Guidelines for Change*) prepared by the National Council for the Social Studies are generally accepted as effective focal themes around which a K–12 program can be planned.

The objectives of the social studies in the Vancouver schools which call for decision-making by pupils are implemented by the use of the problem-solving approach which enables pupils to understand the *why* and the *how* of their surroundings. The core program in the junior high school grades of the University School at the University of Wyoming reveals concern for meaningful use of subject matter through problem-solving techniques.

An examination of the programs of each of the schools presented in Section II reveals either by direct statement or by implication the provision for the achievement of desirable attitudes. Today, as perhaps never before, there is a pledge by the American people regarding values which epitomize the American heritage as these values are examined in the light of a culture greatly affected by new forces from without and from within American society. It remains for each classroom teacher to guide pupils into such learning experiences as will give significance to stated aims of providing for desirable attitudes.

[28] Alexander, William M., *Changing Curriculum Content*. Washington, D.C.: Association for Supervision and Curriculum Development, NEA, 1964, p. 5.
See also:
Gilchrist, Robert S., Ch., *Using Current Curriculum Developments*. Washington, D.C.: Association for Supervision and Curriculum Development, NEA, 1963, p. 74.
Hunt, Herold C., ed., *High School Social Studies Perspectives*. Boston: Houghton, Mifflin Co., 1962.
The Social Studies and the Social Sciences. New York: Harcourt, Brace and World, 1962.
[29] Bruner, Jerome S., *The Process of Education*. Cambridge: Harvard University Press, 1960, pp. 31–32.
[30] Davis, Donald E., *An Analysis of Selected Literature and School Programs for the Determination of Criteria for Curriculum Planning in the Social Studies*. Unpublished Doctoral Dissertation. Laramie, Wyoming: University of Wyoming, 1964, p. 159.
[31] Association for Supervision and Curriculum Development, *A Look at Continuity in the School Program*, 1958 Yearbook. Washington, D.C.: ASCD, NEA, 1958, pp. 128–131.
[32] Ellsworth, Ruth, "Trends in Organization of the Social Studies," *Social Studies in Elementary Schools*, 32nd Yearbook. Washington, D.C.: National Council for the Social Studies, NEA, 1962, p. 124.

Objectives of social studies skills are found in each of the school programs presented in Section II. It would appear unnecessary to review skills which classify under this heading, for they should be apparent in all social studies teaching and learning. A detailed analysis of social studies skills is available for the teacher in the 33rd Yearbook of the National Council for the Social Studies.[33] Perhaps the vital point is that unless these skills are planned for, implemented in teacher-pupil planning, and evaluated in process, they will not be achieved. The ways in which learning may occur become a part of the planned content of the curriculum.

Plan Individual and Group Learning Experiences

The young adolescent is discovering his individuality and at the same time finding much of his life meaning in his group relationships. The educational experience in the junior high years can enhance the democratic ideal very effectively through these two kinds of learning experiences. At University School, Southern Illinois University, committee work and team organization afforded opportunity for the development of valuable group experiences. Individual learning experiences were also planned through oral reports, individually sponsored guests, spelling, and participation in the contests. The learning experiences of an individual and group nature are excellently portrayed by the Setauket plan, where provision for each pupil's learning is continuously planned in great detail within his group level of achievement.

Use Unit Plans Significant to Young Adolescents

From the reading of the school programs in Section II it is evident that in each one, except the Setauket Junior High School, unit planning is the accepted procedure. It is immediately evident, however, that the variation in unit design from that of the teacher-planned unit to that which is developed through teacher-pupil planning reveals the ineffectiveness of objectives which emphasize subject mastery rather than using subject matter to create learning experiences in the form of concepts particularly significant to the young adolescent. When objectives can be stated in terms of

individual experiences, they represent concepts which, as cited earlier in this chapter, form the continuity of learning for the individual. This type of unit planning and objective formulation may be noted in the discussion of unit teaching in the work by Fraser and West.[34] Such a goal does not imply a slipshod classroom or ineffectual teaching. It does not suggest that the whimsical ideas of the young adolescent should be the subject of a class discussion. Careful planning by the alert teacher who knows the aptitudes, interests, and achievements of the pupils in the classroom can arouse pupil interest in problems which are of unique significance to this age level. The classroom atmosphere of open discussion, appreciation by the teacher of each individual pupil, and each pupil's secure relationship within the group can provide the situation for the discovering of exciting, meaningful experience for each learner.

Apply Evolving Instructional Materials, Techniques, and Equipment

The vast array of information materials available today presents a rich resource for the school. In the University School at Southern Illinois University, in the McLoughlin Junior High School, and in the Robinson Junior High School, a basic textbook is cited in the social studies program. However, in each instance, these schools rely upon additional materials. In the Setauket Junior High School several texts are used depending upon the achievement level of the pupils, but again reference is made to many supplementary materials. In the University School at the University of Wyoming no basic textbook is used in the social studies program in the 7th and 8th grades. This review of the selected schools reveals approximately the general situation regarding the use of social studies textbooks in the nation. Need the point be made that the textbook is a tool to assist the teaching-learning situation and as such is but one of many tools? As indicated by the materials pointed out in the Setauket program, the challenge level of materials affords opportunity for meeting individual needs. The numerous commercial sources of audio-visual materials[35] provide a wide coverage of topics or media for the teacher's choice of materials.

[33] Johns, Eunice and Fraser, Dorothy M., "Social Studies Skills: A Guide to Analysis and Grade Placement," *Skill Development in Social Studies*, 33rd Yearbook. Washington, D.C.: National Council for the Social Studies, NEA, 1963, pp. 310–327.

[34] Fraser, Dorothy M. and West, Edith, *Social Studies in the Secondary Schools*. New York: The Ronald Press Co., 1961, pp. 90–100; 114–117.
[35] Hartley, William H., "A Source List of Audio-Visual Materials," *Social Education*, 29:477–479, November, 1965.

With the several mechanical aids to teaching, careful planning in their use will bring a maximum value to the learner. Inappropriate use of the mechanical aid defeats its purpose as a tool for learning. The film, the tape, the transparency on the overhead projector, the kineoscope recording, and the video-tape offer the opportunity for enrichment from vicarious or actual experience, depending upon the device in question. Whatever the supplementary tool, however, thoughtful preparation of the learner prior to using the mechanical aid is essential.[36] Improvements in educational telecasting invite the school to participate in this form of classroom activity. When the classroom teacher can work with the television teacher, an increased opportunity for learning should develop since the television teacher usually has a wide variety of materials and a greater resource for preparation of a telecast.

Evaluate Achievement of Goals

Evaluation is fundamental to a school program, since it appraises the extent to which the objectives of the program are being achieved. Evaluation is concerned with pupil response to the program and reveals the growth of the pupil toward the desired goal. Since it is fundamental to the program, it must be woven into the structure of the teaching-learning situation and is evident in the teacher-pupil planning of units, in the teacher's observation of pupil performance, and in the self-evaluation activities of pupils.

The overall objectives of the K–12 curriculum emphasize the development of the individual. In each of the programs of the five school plans presented in Section II the goal of achieving desirable attitudes, knowledge, and skills in young adolescents is announced. Evaluation is an ongoing process enabling the teacher to decide necessary steps in the teaching-learning situation for each individual's learning. This continuous process is well illustrated in the program at the Setauket Junior High School. Evaluation is an integral part of the program at Southern Illinois University School and in the 7th and 8th grade programs at the University School of the University of Wyoming. Both Robinson Junior High School and McLoughlin Junior High School have expressed beliefs about evaluation and have indicated provision for this phase of their program.

At Setauket, Vancouver, and Wichita it is evident that a sequential development of subject matter is the plan of the social studies program. The formal testing to measure achievement in these programs supplies motivation to many individuals. Where generalizations growing out of pupil experience in using the subject matter have developed and are encompassed by the objectives, the testing should reveal the knowledge or understanding so achieved. Testing should not be a measurement of recall but should be appropriate to a teaching-learning situation which recognizes the needs and interests of young adolescents responding to their cultural environment.

To ascertain the extent to which a program is becoming effective in the behavioral development of pupils requires more than formal testing, valuable as this measurement may be for one portion of the program's objectives. There must be evaluation of social studies skills, of utilization of subject matter, discrimination between fact and opinion, recognition of biased statements and of propaganda, the ability to synthesize information from various disciplines, and to generalize. Helpful suggestions for testing study skills are found in the National Council for the Social Studies Bulletin No. 15, *Selected Items for the Testing of Study Skills and Critical Thinking*.[37]

The objectives of the social studies program involving the development of desirable attitudes present difficulties in evaluation. Teachers will readily admit the difficulty of measuring evidence of pupils' feelings or attitudes. To a considerable extent it must be admitted that an individual's attitudes and feelings are closely related to his knowledge. As Johnson has remarked in Section I, the intellectual development of the individual is the key to his participation in society. Participation must surely be an expression of attitudes, interests, values, and concerns which are the result of generalizations growing out of the individual's learning. To test for citizenship, for ethical values, and for the ideals of character is too difficult, if not impossible, because of the very nature of the qualities under consideration.[38] Checklists, rating scales, and observation by the teacher seem to be most efficient means to evaluate the effectiveness of objectives involving attitudes and values. Use of

---

[36] Refer to National Council for the Social Studies *How To Do It Series* for such titles as "How to Use a Motion Picture," and "How to Use Recordings"; also see Department of Sight and Sound in *Social Education*.

[37] Morse, Horace T. and McCune, George H., *Selected Items for the Testing of Study Skills and Critical Thinking*, Bulletin No. 15. Washington, D.C.: National Council for the Social Studies, NEA, 1957.

[38] Ebel, Robert L., "The Problem of Evaluation in the Social Studies," *Social Education*, 24:6–10, January, 1960.

these devices requires as non-subjective an inter-pretation as possible of the traits being evaluated.

From the checklist used at University School, University of Wyoming, concern for desirable atti-tudes is reflected in the section headed Social and Emotional Development with the following items listed:

1. Is courteous and cooperative
2. Respects rights of others
3. Gets along well with others
4. Respects authority
5. Shows growth in self-control
6. Accepts responsibility

These items are rated in the following scale: Out-standing, Satisfactory, Improving, Not Improving.

A continuous evaluation of the program of learning should maintain effective procedures for the attainment of the stated goals. A significant factor in this process is the teacher's planning and evaluating of classroom activities in which young adolescents find meaningful concepts for them-selves. A social studies curriculum which is based upon significant concepts developed through units growing out of the personal-social and social-civic needs of young adolescents should afford a sequen-tial learning and development for the individual.

How May Teacher-School-Community Relations Contribute to Improved Social Studies Instruction?

The day has passed when the curriculum and its implementation were solely the responsibility of the school, when education was "something that occurred within the walls of the classroom." Par-ents who are deeply involved in the problems of the young adolescents in their families and lay-men who plan and work for the maintenance of a desirable community can be helpfully engaged in school affairs. When laymen and parents are fre-quent visitors in the school helping teachers and administrators with a variety of projects which provide the developmental experiences of young adolescents, there will be less need for special campaigns to inform the public about school problems, or to win approval for some curriculum revision.

School Objectives and Procedures Are Established by Cooperative Staff Effort

In its broadest sense the junior high school pro-vides social learning for young adolescents. The attitudes, values, tastes, and appreciations which are the outcomes of education for an adult society cannot be achieved in total in the junior high

school, but a direction toward these developmental maturings may be pointed. It is essential that the design of the social studies program for the young adolescent be based upon objectives specific and practical enough to be meaningful and dynamic in influence to the learner, the teacher, and the com-munity. We read from Lounsbury in Section I that objectives must guide the experiences of the young adolescent actively, not leaving to casual assump-tion that the specific values, attitudes, skills, and understandings will result somehow.

Planning the program in social studies must be the work of a team consisting of administra-tors, curriculum coordinators, classroom teachers, school patrons, and pupils. These individuals with adequate time provided for consultation must examine the local scene as it bears upon the young adolescent. The question they must resolve is how the young adolescent can best be served as he lives and grows in this community. Such a ques-tion recognizes the individual in his present state of maturation and relationships and sees him as an individual with purposes, ambitions, and needs for present and future fulfillment.

The pupil is readily engaged in adapting the curriculum to his needs and interests as each teacher shares with pupils the planning of units of work which compose the scope of the program. Teacher-pupil planning is an essential technique in the classroom if individuals are to learn in their own sequential development.

To keep the individual learner uppermost in consideration for curriculum planning, it is neces-sary that the classroom teacher be an integral part of the planning, of the formulating of objectives, and of the selection of subject matter which will be the vehicle for the learning situations. Occa-sionally curriculum revision is the work of a se-lected group of supervisors and consultants who produce a "guide" to be followed by the teachers of a local system. Unless the classroom teacher has shared in the decisions and choices which are incorporated in the "guide," there is little chance that the teachers will use the "guide" effectively. The teacher grows through the in-service experi-ence of consulting and planning with other teachers, of becoming aware of the total curricu-lum. The importance of the classroom teacher in the planning of the curriculum is cited by Crowe,[39] who recognizes the need for the teacher to under-

---

[39] Department of Elementary School Principals, *Focus on the Social Studies*, A Report from the Dept. of Ele-mentary School Principals' Annual Meeting. Washington, D.C.: NEA, 1965, p. 49.

stand the nature of the content chosen for the curriculum.

At Southern Illinois University School a long term project of social studies planning has seen teachers from all grades working together with assistance from a resource consultant. That the individual pupil has been the immediate concern in this school's effort to establish suitable aims for the social studies program can be seen by a review of the objectives. Within the objectives are included the ideas for immediate application and for long term development.

In Vancouver, Washington, teachers and a resource consultant set up the objectives and planned units to compose a guide for use in the Vancouver classrooms. Pupils were considered in their present stage of growth in such objectives as to make decisions of their own, to respect and appreciate other races, religions, minorities, nations, and cultures. Objectives recognizing not only the present but a future level of achievement based on present developmental experiences are "to create an awareness of man's economic interdependence and an understanding of the free enterprise system," "to understand problems which arise because of growth in population, mobility of people, technological advancements, business expansion, and governmental functions," "to develop an awareness and understanding of the active conflict between the two major ideologies in the world today," "to understand the importance of our natural resources."

In the Wichita "guide" for the social studies we find the result of work of many individuals engaged in curriculum study for the city schools, among whom were teachers from each grade level. The "guide" is considered to be a resource for use by all teachers in their own planning although all teachers of the social studies did not apparently share in the curriculum study.

From these programs it is evident that schools are aware of the need for cooperative planning of objectives and content in the social studies program. Since planning must be an ongoing process, it will doubtless become evident to those interested in the improvement of instruction that each classroom teacher must share in the combined effort of curriculum evaluation and revision.

Social Studies Teachers Plan Learning Experiences in Relation to Scope and Sequence of Kindergarten Through Grade 12

Schools vary in the attention given to curriculum planning which recognizes the range of development of the individual from the kindergarten through the 12th grade. This range of development is the sequence of learning which is unique for each learner within the general experience of his class or grade level. The learning which a teacher plans is guided by two factors, the scope and sequence. By scope is indicated the breadth of subject matter and by sequence is meant the articulation from grade to grade. The scope of the program reflects the objectives and adapts the experiences to the readiness of the pupil. In the junior high school a fairly wide difference can exist among pupils in their degrees of readiness for some learning experiences. Hence, it is evident that a program should be flexible enough to vary the scope in terms of each learner rather than arbitrarily establishing required subject matter at a given grade level. We cannot set up a curriculum for a "typical 7th grader" or a "typical 8th grader," since these averages are fictitious.

As previously indicated, the philosophy of the school personnel and community determines the program of the school. Since not everything can be taught, selection of content must occur. In the social studies K–12 there should be a decision as to the general scope such as that suggested in the *Guide to Content in the Social Studies*. There will always be community pressures as well as legal requirements concerning the curriculum content. In the democratic society a wide range of values necessitates a consensus in curriculum planning so that common values of greatest worth can be recognized. The classroom teacher will carry further the decision and selection of content at each grade level. The values chosen must obviously become the determining influences on the learning experiences of the individual pupils.

The listed themes for each succeeding grade level should afford the opportunity for the overall objectives of the school to be achieved. The objectives, if stated by grades, as at University School, University of Wyoming, should be part of the K–12 list, and the experiences at each grade level contribute to the eventual, total achievement. The articulated, sequential experience of themes such as the social concepts emphasized in the Southern Illinois University School sequence and in that of the Vancouver schools, provides for reinforcement of learning and enables the individual pupil to follow his own interest drives under teacher advisement and to discover new challenges of learning as the teacher-pupil planning implements the proposed theme or problems to be considered at each grade level.

A review of the statements of sequence among the school programs in Section II reveals that the theory of widening horizons is followed frequently. Other types of sequential planning are found among revised curriculum designs. The spiral plan permits repetition of a topic at chosen grade levels to allow a broader experience at successively high grades. The valid implications of the theory of developmental tasks suggest the very appropriate use of maturation and readiness as keys to the planning of sequence. Whatever plan is followed by a school, the sequential development should be articulated to implement the overall objectives of the school.

Resource Units Are Constructed by Social Studies Staff

Instruction in the social studies can be greatly improved by the use of resource units as these bodies of material supply ideas and suggestions for teachers in planning their own teaching units. Since resource units are for teachers, they should be constructed by teachers. All the social studies teachers of the staff should participate in the work of building the resource unit. Since the resource unit is very broad in its content relating to a given topic, the objectives and learning activities proposed will be extensive. Several teachers planning such a resource together do contribute valuable elements to the unit as well as exchanging worthwhile ideas of relating content to learning. A depth of knowledge of subject matter for the resource unit is essential.

Objectives classified as knowledge, attitudes, and skills should be listed with knowledge objectives stated as generalizations. Attitudes objectives may seem difficult to distinguish from factual content; however, these objectives should emphasize the element of feeling or ideal which results from the fact. Skill objectives associated with the resource unit should be specific.

The learning activities listed will suggest the things teachers may do to initiate and carry through a teaching unit. Activities for the learner will be listed and ways in which the teaching unit may be closed will be included. The closing activities must continue the learning process and as such do relate to the objectives listed in the resource unit.

The resource unit is valuable in helping teachers free themselves from a textbook. When all the teachers on the staff participate in the building of resource units, the value of each teacher in "thinking through" the items of the resource unit is apparent.

Community Life is Recognized by Teachers, Parents, and Pupils in Curriculum Planning

Important as the role of the social studies is in the educational program, the school is concerned with the whole child, the child with all his interests and concerns which contribute to his learning. This fact necessitates a close cooperation between the school and the community, the inclusive environment in which the child lives. While the social studies emphasize human relationships and involve social-civic institutions in the program, it remains the responsibility of the entire staff of the junior high school to maintain a constructive interaction with the community.

Among the schools cited in Section II, community resource persons are noted as the possible relation of school and community as well as field trips to local enterprises. When young adolescents participate in local campaigns of a type to build social consciousness, those objectives which point toward democratic attitudes are being implemented. Even more effective for the achievement of the aims of the school is the informal sharing by parents and other laymen in school projects which call for adult participation, such as chaperoning social activities, accompanying groups on trips, assisting with projects, driving cars where special transportation is needed, and assisting teachers with tasks which may be delegated by them. When the citizens of a community work with young adolescents in projects and activities of their life, a greater understanding is mutually possible and many worthwhile attitudes develop. True cooperation means a growth and increased understanding for all the parties concerned.

Selected References

1. Alexander, William M., *Changing Curriculum Content.* Washington, D. C.: Association for Supervision and Curriculum Development, NEA, 1964, p. 5.
2. Association for Supervision and Curriculum Development, *Individualizing Instruction*, 1964 Yearbook. Washington, D. C.: ASCD, NEA, 1964, p. 92.
3. Association for Supervision and Curriculum Development, *The Junior High School We Need.* Washington, D. C.: Report from ASCD Commission on Secondary Education, NEA, 1961, p. 3.
4. Association for Supervision and Curriculum Development, *A Look at Continuity in the*

School Program, 1958 Yearbook. Washington, D. C.: ASCD, NEA, 1958, pp. 128–131.

5. Association for Supervision and Curriculum Development, *New Insights and The Curriculum.* Washington, D. C.: ASCD, NEA, 1963, pp. 122–123, 239.

6. Berelson, Bernard, and others, *The Social Studies and The Social Sciences.* New York: Harcourt, Brace and World, 1962.

7. Bruner, Jerome S., *The Process of Education.* Cambridge: Harvard University Press, 1960, pp. 31–32.

8. Center for the Study of Instruction, *Current Curriculum Studies in Academic Subjects.* Washington, D.C.: NEA, 1962, p. 73.

9. Cottle, Eugene, "The Core Class Encourages Democratic Skills," *Wyoming Education News*, 23:9–10, 22, November, 1956.

10. Davis, Donald E., *An Analysis of Selected Literature and School Programs for the Determination of Criteria for Curriculum Planning in the Social Studies.* Unpublished Doctoral Dissertation. Laramie: University of Wyoming, 1964, p. 159.

11. Department of Elementary School Principals, *Focus on the Social Studies* (Report from the Department of Elementary School Principal's Annual Meeting). Washington, D. C.: NEA, 1965, p. 49.

12. Dewey, John, *Democracy and Education.* New York: Macmillan, 1916, pp. 89–90.

13. Ebel, Robert L., "The Problem of Evaluation in the Social Studies," *Social Education*, 24: 6–10, January, 1960.

14. Ellsworth, Ruth, "Trends in Organization of the Social Studies," *Social Studies in Elementary Schools.* Washington, D. C.: National Council for the Social Studies, NEA, 1962, p. 124.

15. Fenton, Edwin, *Teaching the New Social Studies in Secondary Schools.* New York: Holt, Rinehart and Winston, Inc., 1966, pp. 348–365.

16. Fraser, Dorothy M., "Status and Expectations of Current Research and Development Projects," *Social Education*, 29:421–434, November, 1965.

17. Fraser, Dorothy M., and McCutcheon, Samuel P., *Social Studies in Transition: Guidelines for Change*, Curriculum Series No. 12. Washington, D.C.: National Council for the Social Studies, 1965.

18. Fraser, Dorothy M. and West, Edith, *Social Studies in Secondary Schools.* New York: The Ronald Press Co., 1961, p. 90.

19. Gilchrist, Robert S., Ch., *Using Current Curriculum Developments.* Washington, D. C.: Association for Supervision and Curriculum Development, NEA, 1963, p. 74.

20. Goodlad, John I., *School Curriculum Reform in the United States.* New York: The Fund for the Advancement of Education, 1964, p. 42.

21. Gross, Richard E., Muessig, R. H., and Fersh, G. L., eds., *The Problems Approach and the Social Studies*, Curriculum Series No. 9. Washington, D. C.: National Council for the Social Studies, NEA, 1960.

22. Halversen, Paul M., Ch., *Balance in the Curriculum*, 1961 Yearbook. Washington, D. C.: Association for Supervision and Curriculum Development, NEA, 1961, pp. 10–15.

23. Hartley, William H., "A Source List of Audio-Visual Materials," *Social Education*, 29:477–479, November, 1965.

24. Havighurst, Robert J., *Developmental Tasks and Education.* New York: Longmans, Green and Co., 1952.

25. Herriott, M. E., Sands, Elizabeth, and Stauffacher, Harry W., "History and Objectives of Junior High Education in California," *Bulletin of the National Association of Secondary School Principals*, 31:14–19, December, 1951.

26. Hunt, Herold C., ed., *High School Social Studies Perspectives.* Boston: Houghton, Mifflin Co., 1962.

27. Lindsey, Margaret, "Decision-Making and the Teacher," *Curriculum Crossroads.* Columbia University, New York: Teachers College Press, Teachers College, 1962, pp. 27–40.

28. Michaelis, John U., "Social Studies," *Using Current Curriculum Developments.* Washington, D. C.: The Association for Supervision and Curriculum Development, 1963, p. 73.

29. Mooney, Ross L., *Mooney Problems Checklist, Form J.* Columbus, Ohio: Bureau of Educational Research, Ohio State University, 1950.

30. Morse, Horace T., and McCune, George H., *Selected Items for the Testing of Study Skills and Critical Thinking*, Bulletin No. 15. Washington, D.C.: National Council for the Social Studies, NEA, 1957.

31. National Council for the Social Studies, *How To Do It Series.*

32. National Council for the Social Studies, "The Role of the Social Studies," *Social Education*, 26:315, October, 1962.

33. Rice, Marion J., and Bailey, Wilfred C., "A Sequential Curriculum in Anthropology for Grades 1–7," *Social Education*, 29:211–212, April, 1965.

34. Samford, Clarence D., and Cottle, Eugene, *Social Studies in the Secondary School.* New York: McGraw-Hill Book Co., Inc., 1952, pp. 320–341.

35. *Social Education*, "Department of Sight and Sound."

36. *The Social Studies and the Social Sciences.* American Council of Learned Societies. New York: Harcourt, Brace and World, Inc., 1962.

37. Vancouver Public Schools, *Program of Social Studies.*

38. Wichita Public School System, *Personnel Policies for the Classroom Teacher.* Wichita, Kansas: September 16, 1963.